'*Rebel Financing and Terrorism in Civil Wars* is a great book on a highly important topic. It is a must-read for anyone interested in civil war, terrorism, or the funding of militant organizations.'

Brian J Phillips, *University of Essex, UK*

'*Rebel Financing and Terrorism in Civil Wars* brings together several literatures to produce a comprehensive analysis of the link between rebel group financing and strategic use of terrorism. Using both case studies and quantitative data, Belgioioso investigates different sets of financing actors and her conclusions both reinforce and challenge conventional wisdoms on armed group financing patterns and the nature of violence groups engage in. The book is a valuable resource for anyone interested in understanding rebel financing, rebel constituencies, and rebel use of terrorism in civil conflicts.'

James A. Piazza, *Liberal Arts Professor of Political Science, The Pennsylvania State University, USA*

'Belgioioso argues that how rebellion is financed strongly impacts the incentives of dissidents to resort to terrorist attacks. Terrorist tactics are often logistically easier but can undermine domestic legitimacy through harm to civilians. However, Belgioioso shows that such costs figure less prominently when rebel groups have access to external and more diverse financing, which makes them less reliant on local support. Belgioioso also identifies the impact of various sources of financing that were previously not studied in the literature. This book underscores the value of identifying variation in sources of funding and substitution, and it deserves to be read by all those interested in rebel tactic choice and civilian victimization.'

Kristian Skrede Gleditsch, *University of Essex, UK, and Peace Research Institute Oslo, Norway*

'Belgioioso convincingly demonstrates that the sources of finance for insurgent groups affect their targeting of civilians with terrorist attacks. *Rebel Financing and Terrorism in Civil Wars* offers rich theoretical arguments employing sophisticated statistical analysis and detailed case studies with profound policy implications.'

Scott Gates, *Research Professor, Peace Research Institute Oslo, Norway*

Rebel Financing and Terrorism in Civil Wars

This book investigates the ways in which the lethality of terrorist violence depends on how rebel organizations finance their rebellion.

The leaders of rebel groups make calculated decisions on the intensity of terrorism killings, considering the benefits and costs of targeting non-combatants against the financing needs of their organization. The study specifically focuses on analyzing the effects of different external financing options available to rebel groups and takes into account the role of local populations in making financing available. This comparative approach to external financing reveals new hypotheses that are empirically verified and differ from the expectations and findings of prior research. The book's findings are relevant to policy discussions on counter-insurgency strategies that prioritize protecting populations from human rights abuses. Existing doctrines tend to overlook the potential impact of targeted efforts to isolate insurgents from specific financing sources on the capacity to secure local populations.

This book will be of interest to students of civil wars, terrorism studies, political violence, and security studies.

Margherita Belgioioso is Lecturer in Quantitative International Relations, at the University of Leeds, UK.

Routledge Studies in Civil Wars and Intra-State Conflict

Series editors: Edward Newman, *School of Politics and International Studies, University of Leeds, UK*; and *Idean Salehyan, University of North Texas, USA.*

This series publishes theoretically rigorous and empirically original scholarship on all aspects of armed intrastate conflict, including its causes, nature, impacts, patterns of violence, and resolution. It welcomes work on specific armed conflicts and the micro-dynamics of violence, on broad patterns and cross-national analyses of civil wars, and on historical perspectives as well as contemporary challenges. It also seeks to explore the policy implications of conflict analysis, especially as it relates to international security, intervention, and peacebuilding.

Foreign Intervention, Warfare and Civil Wars
External Assistance and Belligerents' Choice of Strategy
Adam Lockyer

Armed Groups and International Legitimacy
Child Soldiers in Intra-State Conflict
William Plowright

Partition and Peace in Civil Wars
Dividing Lands and Peoples to End Ethnic Conflict
Carter R. Johnson

Militias, States and Violence against Civilians
Civic Vice, Civic Virtue
Edited by Paul Lorenzo Johnson and William Wittels

For more information about this series, please visit: www.routledge.com/Routledge-Studies-in-Civil-Wars-and-Intra-State-Conflict/book-series/CIVILWARS

Rebel Financing and Terrorism in Civil Wars

Margherita Belgioioso

Routledge
Taylor & Francis Group
LONDON AND NEW YORK

First published 2024
by Routledge
4 Park Square, Milton Park, Abingdon, Oxon OX14 4RN

and by Routledge
605 Third Avenue, New York, NY 10158

Routledge is an imprint of the Taylor & Francis Group, an informa business

British Library Cataloguing-in-Publication Data
A catalogue record for this book is available from the British Library

ISBN: 978-1-032-44501-4 (hbk)
ISBN: 978-1-032-45464-1 (pbk)
ISBN: 978-1-003-37713-9 (ebk)

DOI: 10.4324/9781003377139

Typeset in Times New Roman
by Newgen Publishing UK

Contents

Figures

Introduction

For nearly two decades, the Abu Sayyaf Group (ASG) waged an armed campaign in the southern islands of the Philippines, seeking to establish an independent Islamic state and assert the rights of the Muslim minority against the Catholic-led central government. Throughout this period, the group's primary means of violence were highly deadly indiscriminate bombings of civilian targets and kidnappings of foreign tourists, which resulted in a tragic toll of 456 civilian deaths (Abuza 2002) and extensive media coverage (Hiranandani 2006). However, from the mid-1990s onwards, ASG underwent a dramatic shift in its tactics and strategic objectives. The organization began to question the effectiveness of terrorist killings and turned to more discriminate kidnap-for-ransom attacks and other violent criminal activities against government officials and local businesses (Abuza 2002; Banoldi 2010). This shift in violence is believed to be linked to the loss of external support from Al-Qaeda (Abuza 2002, 190). Similar tactical shifts took place in the cases of the United Liberation Front of Assam in India, the Tamil Tigers in Sri Lanka, and the Irish Republican Army in the United Kingdom. Even though understanding the role of financing sources and supporters of rebel groups in civil wars is likely to have important implications for conflict transformation and even resolution, there is a lack of analysis on the ways in which different financing methods shape the lethality of terrorist campaigns carried out by militant groups in civil wars.

This book aims to explore the impact of rebel group financing on the intensity of terrorist violence – the deliberate use of violence by non-state actors against non-combatant targets to achieve a

DOI: 10.4324/9781003377139-1

political goal through the intimidation of a wider audience beyond the immediate victims – employed by dissident groups during civil wars. To this end, I depart from the key assumption that the leadership cadres of rebel organizations take rational decisions on the intensity of terrorism killings, weighing the benefits and the costs of targeting non-combatants with terrorist attacks against the financing needs of their organization. In order for a rebel organization to be viable, it must possess the ability to withstand the military might of its government's army. This involves the maintenance of manpower and equipment and, therefore, requires resources (Collier et al. 1999; Hazen 2013). The financing of rebel groups is commonly sourced either 'internally' through local popular support or 'externally' through means such as natural resource exploitation, foreign state backing, and support from external non-state organizations (Collier et al. 1999). Practitioners and academics widely agree that the means by which rebel groups finance their violent campaigns determine – at least in part – the scope and nature of their violent tactics in civil wars. However, despite the significant amount of research on rebel financing and dynamics of violence, the relative importance of specific sources of external financing available to rebels and the impact of external financing source diversity on the decision to employ lethal terrorist violence have been largely overlooked in the existing literature. The effect of the support provided by different external non-state actors on the severity of terrorist violence during civil wars has also not been systematically studied. This monograph seeks to address these gaps in the current literature and examine the relevance of its findings for counter-insurgency operations.

The field of Conflict Studies has witnessed a growing body of empirical research indicating that terrorist attacks are not only more frequent but also more lethal during civil wars. Moreover, global surges in terrorist attacks appear to stem from an increased use of terrorism in complex and increasingly internationalized civil conflicts (Belgioioso 2018; Clauset and Gleditsch 2012; Findley and Young 2012; Fortna 2015; Polo and Gleditsch 2016; Stanton 2013; Thomas 2014). Traditional accounts in the field of Terrorism Studies have tended to examine the causes and severity of terrorism in isolation from other forms of political violence. Yet, evidence suggests that various violent political behaviours may complement each other rather than serve exclusively as substitutes. The extent to which rebel groups employ terrorist violence against non-combatants as a complement to more conventional warfare tactics, for example, varies across rebel groups and may also change over time (Asal et al. 2015; Findley and Young 2012; Sanchez-Cuenca and De La Calle 2009). This observation led to a surge in research that compares rebel groups using both conventional and terrorist violence to those solely employing conventional violence, with the aim of better understanding the factors influencing the intensity and lethality of terrorist attacks. This approach is grounded in the notion that analysing the factors that make terrorism appealing to a rational non-state actor given certain structural characteristics alone is inadequate in explaining the incidence and deadliness of terrorist attacks. To provide a more coherent empirical evaluation of the rationalist explanation of terrorism, it is necessary to consider why non-state actors are unable to identify alternative dissident strategies or outcomes that they would prefer over terrorism (Belgioioso 2018; Polo and González 2020, 2035).

Empirical works on terrorism in the context of civil wars have, to date, predominantly concentrated on the impact of rebel group traits, including ideology, military might, and size, as well as conflict dynamics, such as inter-rebel factional competition, and structural factors, including regime type and media freedom (Asal and Rethemeyer 2008; Belgioioso 2018; Belgioioso and Thurber 2023; Kalyvas 2006; Kydd and Walter 2006; Polo and Gleditsch 2016; Stanton 2013; Wood 2010). Existing research has shown that terrorist attacks are more prevalent among militarily disadvantaged rebel groups in civil wars (Polo and Gleditsch 2016; Wood 2010) and that terrorism is more lethal and indiscriminate against civilians when rebel organizations carrying out the attacks espouse ethnic separatist and/or religious ideologies (Asal and Rethemeyer 2008; Polo and Gleditsch 2016). Specific conflict dynamics also appear relevant for shaping the cost–benefit calculation of using terrorism in civil wars. Existing literature indicates that internal and external pressures on rebel groups encourage the use of terrorist attacks. Growing followers' fatigue over time and progressive fragmentation of rebel organizations involved in civil conflicts increase the likelihood of terrorist campaigns onsets (Belgioioso 2018). The occurrence of anti-pluralist ideologies also encourages the use of terrorist attacks during civil wars by shaping dynamics of competition between rebel organizations (Belgioioso and Thurber 2023). There is also evidence that rebels that need of rallying civilian support when they suffer severe military losses and there is a history of indiscriminate government repression, are also incentivize the use of terrorism (Polo and González 2020). Finally, there is evidence that rebels in civil wars use terrorism more intensely when they face violent and repressive regimes, can exploit democratic regimes' rule of law, and have more opportunities for media dissemination in states where press freedom is more protected (Polo and González 2020; Stanton 2013).

Although this literature and its theoretical framework has made a decisive contribution for our understanding of terrorism as a tactic of dissent rather than as sui generis, irrational event, some important questions remain unanswered. The relationship between the financing of rebel groups and the severity of terrorist violence they employ has yet to be thoroughly investigated. Indeed, besides Fortna et al.'s (2018) finding that rebels' exploitation of natural resources increases the probability of terrorism occurrence in civil wars, there remains a dearth of conclusive empirical research on how the severity of terrorist violence employed by rebel organizations in civil conflicts is associated with their diverse financing strategies. Arguably, comprehending the factors that contribute to the severity of terrorist attacks is more critical for counter-insurgency operations than understanding the factors that drive the adoption of terrorist tactics. This is because a significant proportion of reported terrorist incidents do not result in any fatalities (Fortna et al. 2018), and the level of threat posed by rebel organizations to states through terrorism is commonly linked to the intensity and lethality of these attacks (Newman 2007, 473). According to this conceptualization of threat level, a developing body of literature has examined how rebels' financing influences the severity of violence that goes beyond conventional attacks on state coercive apparatuses, with a particular focus on civilian victimization during civil wars. This literature posits that rebel groups with external resources, be it from foreign governments, external non-state entities, or obtained through the exploitation of natural resources, are less dependent on local communities for support, which in turn leads to more brutal violence against civilians (Hovil and Werker 2005; Humphreys and Weinstein 2006; Lujala 2009;

Salehyan et al. 2014; Toft and Zhukov 2015; Weinstein 2007; Whitaker et al. 2019; R. M. Wood 2014).

Within this literature, there is evidence that when rebels are less reliant on the local population, such as in the case of Jihadist organizations, government repression is less effective in preventing rebel violence against civilians (Toft and Zhukov 2015). These studies have also found that widespread civilian abuse, which includes looting, sexual violence, mass killings, and other forms of violent coercion, has occurred more severely when rebels had weaker ethnic ties with the local population and were financially supported by foreign state sponsors or natural resources (Humphreys and Weinstein 2006; Weinstein 2007). Existing literature also suggests that conflict intensity, measured by the total number of combat-related deaths, including civilian casualties, tends to be higher in areas with abundant natural resources such as gemstones, oil, and gas (Lujala 2009). Furthermore, the decision of rebel groups to either make use of or refrain from civilian victimization can function as a powerful signalling mechanism to attract or retain financing from specific external supporters. For instance, Hovil and Werker's (2005) analysis of the failed rebellion of the Allied Democratic Forces (ADF) in western Uganda shows that the ADF's use of civilian victimization was an attempt to signal credibility and maintain the support of external supporters such as Mobutu's Zaire, the Sudanese government, Al-Qaeda, and other radical Islamists. Similarly, Salehyan et al. (2014) find that the probability of rebels using one-sided violence in civil wars decreases when they finance their rebellion through external support from democratic states with strong human rights lobbies.

In addition to these studies, there is a substantial body of qualitative research that examines the impact of diaspora communities on the dynamics of civil wars. Specifically, it investigates whether diaspora support for insurgent groups in their countries of origin affects the perpetuation of the conflict or the promotion of peacebuilding efforts. The literature on global governance, as well as works investigating the actions of diaspora groups in the context of civil wars, has often associated diaspora communities with a tendency to support the continuation of hostilities and to undermine attempts to reach negotiated settlements and promote peaceful reconciliation (Anderson 2019; Duffield 2002,

153–65; Kaldor 2012). This literature highlights a crucial aspect for this book, which is the demonstrated ability of external non-state actors, including diaspora and NGOs, not only to promote the political goals of militant groups in their receiving countries but also to mobilize financial resources, supply military personnel, and provide weaponry directly to rebel groups in their countries of origin. Nonetheless, the findings of the current body of qualitative research examining the impact of external non-state actors' backing of rebel groups in their respective homelands are inconclusive and, at times, conflicting. While some studies suggest that diaspora support impedes the resolution of civil conflicts, several other qualitative case studies highlight the constructive role played by diaspora supporters of rebels in ending conflicts and reducing the level of violence perpetrated by rebel groups against civilians. For instance, Cochrane et al. (2009) document the Irish-American diaspora's efforts to directly engage with militant Irish republicans, who relied heavily on the diaspora's financial support and encouraged them to adopt a more peaceful and democratic agenda (695). Fair (2005) similarly demonstrates that the Tamil diaspora, which served as the primary financing source for the Liberation Tigers of Tamil Eelam (LTTE), pressured the group to adopt more moderate positions and engage in peace talks with the Sri Lankan government. This pressure stemmed from the Tamil diaspora's increasing unease with the LTTE's use of suicide bombings and the forcible recruitment of children.

In summary, while there is a growing body of literature examining the impact of rebels' natural resources exploitation and foreign state support on civilian victimization and civil war violence, as well as a rich corpus of qualitative case studies exploring the role of diaspora groups in shaping civil wars dynamics of violence and termination, we do not possess systematic knowledge on the role that diversity of external financing methods plays when it comes to terrorism killings. We are also left without a systematic understanding of the comparative effects of different sources of external financing on the decision of rebel groups to use lethal terrorist violence. Finally, while the effects of financing provided by different external state actors on civilian victimization have received attention, the effect of financing provided by different types of non-state supporters remains systematically unexplored. In contrast to existing works, this book adopts a comparative perspective on the role of various sources of financing available to rebel groups in civil wars.

This study's theoretical analysis specifically focuses on examining and comparing the impact of different external financing options available to rebel groups on the severity of terrorist violence, while taking into account the local population's role in facilitating access to each type of external financing. This comparative approach to external financing yields new, empirically verifiable hypotheses that differ from those advanced in previous research. First, I hypothesize that rebels that receive financing from external non-state groups and foreign states are equally unconstrained when committing terrorist violence against non-combatants. Second, I hypothesize that rebels that finance their armed campaigns through the exploitation of natural resources incur a higher cost in terms of legitimacy when it comes to terrorism killings, compared to rebels financing their armed campaigns through the support of foreign states and external non-state actors. This latter hypothesis has implications for rebels' use of terrorist killings that contradict the expectations of existing studies (Fortna et al. 2018). Specifically, I expect that rebel groups that sustain their armed campaign through natural resources exploitation limit the lethality of terrorist attacks when compared to rebels that rely on foreign states and external non-state actors. This is because the exploitation of natural resources is location specific and dependent on some level of compliance from the local population. From an empirical point of view, this study is the first that compares the effects and magnitude of different types of external financing sources on rebels' violence. While the majority of rebel groups exploit only one source of external financing, for a large minority of rebel organizations, available resources derive from a mixture of various external sources of financing (around 20% in my sample). A theoretical and empirical analysis on the role of diversity of external financing sources on the lethality of terrorism in civil war also sets this study apart from existing works. Finally, this study is the first to analyse the effects of the support of different types of external non-state actors. Since the end of the Cold War, external non-state actors such as diasporas, foreign NGOs, and external rebel movements have gained a prominent role in fostering and sustaining rebel groups. I develop and test novel principal-agent propositions that explain how the lethality of terrorist violence varies depending on the goals that specific types of non-state organizations have when financing a rebellion. By comparing the effect of different external financing sources available to rebels and focusing on the impact of different types of external non-state supporters, this chapter advances a more nuanced and comprehensive understanding of how rebels shape the tactical choice of terrorism killings in civil wars depending on the ways in which they finance their rebellion. Finally, this book uses new data on external financing coded by the author.

The overreaching argument of this book is that rebel groups targeting non-combatants with terrorist attacks must consider the potential costs of this tactic. These costs mainly concern the alienation of local popular supporters. The reliance on external financing, especially from foreign states and external non-state organizations compared to natural resources, and on more diverse external financing sources decreases the impact of local legitimacy costs associated with terrorism. A lower salience of the local legitimacy costs associated with terrorist attacks, in turn, tends to lead rebel groups to perpetrate more intense terrorism killings than more intense conventional violence. Terrorism, which involves targeting civilians, is less costly militarily compared to conventional warfare activities, but it can help advance rebels' positions (Thomas 2014) and goals (Muro 2020). The impact of external non-state actors' support on the lethality of terrorist attacks is comparable to that of foreign states' support because rebel groups face similar legitimacy costs when relying on any external actors, as opposed to direct support from local populations or the exploitation of location-specific natural resources. The effect of financing from external non-state actors on the lethality of terrorism, however, is likely to vary depending on the specific interests of the non-state supporter. Financing from diasporas and NGOs is likely to decrease the use of lethal terrorist violence against non-combatants because these groups typically support rebels in their home countries with the goal of minimizing insecurity and shaping favourable long-term political outcomes for the local population. Financing from external rebel groups, on the contrary, is likely to increase the lethality of terrorist violence as armed groups support rebels in other countries to assert their international and local political influence and see highly lethal terrorist attacks as a measure of the credible commitment of their rebel protégées.

I test these expectations against data on 204 rebel groups in civil wars from 1989 to 2009. My dataset contains information on the lethality of terrorist attacks against non-combatants and the lethality of conventional violence against combatants, together with information on rebels' various financing sources. The comparative focus of this study on individual financing sources, financing sources diversity, and types of non-state supporters calls for new data. There is an important research tradition on external support to rebel groups that relies on well-established data sources such as the UCDP External Support Project – Primary Warring Party Dataset (Högbladh et al. 2011) and the recently released UCDP external support dataset (ESD), 1975–2017 (Meier et al. 2022). However, the former does not directly disaggregate data on the basis of the sources of financing and the latter only contains information limited to support by foreign governments and external rebels. Additionally, these and similar datasets impose restrictions that make them unsuitable to study the comparative and cumulative effects of external financing methods that I focus on in this book. Therefore, building on the textual information contained in the UCDP External Support Project – Primary Warring Party Dataset (Högbladh et al. 2011) and on qualitative academic research on rebels' financing methods, I code new data on sources of financing. The empirical analysis demonstrates that while rebels with more diverse external sources of financing perpetrate more intense terrorism killings, the support of foreign states and external non-state actors similarly increases the lethality of terrorist violence. To the contrary, the effect of natural resources exploitation on terrorism lethality is not distinguishable from the effect of financing obtained through the support of the local population. This is because rebels that rely on natural resources are more subjected to local legitimacy costs than those that rely on external actors. Overall, these findings highlight the importance of exploring systematically the so far under-investigated role of external non-state supporters to comprehend the dynamics of violence in civil wars. In this regard, the empirical analysis shows that financing from diasporas and NGOs decreases terrorism lethality while financing from external rebel groups encourages terrorism killings. Crucially, diasporas and NGOs have preferences to provide support to rebel groups that avoid indiscriminate terrorist violence, while external rebel groups perceive more lethal terrorist violence carried out by their rebel protégées as a signal of credible commitment to armed rebellion.

This study is relevant to inform policy discussions on counter-insurgency strategies such as the ones contained in the Allied Joint Doctrine for Counter-Insurgency operations of NATO (COIN). Counter-insurgency strategies targeted at protecting the populations from human rights abuses and crimes against humanity emphasize the importance of external support for the sustainment of insurgencies. However, while it is recognized that breaking lines of communication between rebel groups and their external sources of financing makes insurgents vulnerable and that insurgents' inability to gain external financing may impact their capability to sustain campaigns, existing doctrines fail to fully recognize the potential impact of more targeted efforts to isolate insurgents from specific sources of financing on the ability to secure the local population. According to my expectations, the empirical findings show that not all external financing methods bear the same effect on the level of threat from terrorist attacks. The results of the empirical analysis suggest that, if the primary focus on counter-insurgency operations is to increase the security of the local population, efforts to isolate rebels from their sources of financing should proceed according to the level of threat that different financing methods imply. First, since support from foreign states and external rebel groups correlates with more intense terrorism killings, isolating rebels from these financing sources should be given priority over isolating them from diaspora and NGOs or from the access to natural resources. Second, my findings suggest that counter-insurgency operations might actually benefit from diplomatic efforts that make diaspora and NGOs part of political solutions to civil conflicts.

This book is divided into five principal chapters. The first chapter characterizes terrorism as one of the contentious political behaviours available to dissident organizations in armed conflicts and compares the tactical benefits of targeting non-combatants with terrorist violence against the direct target of state coercive apparatuses. Chapter 1 also discusses how intentionally targeting non-combatants with terrorism carries the risk of alienating the audiences of rebel groups, resulting in significant costs in terms of popular support and legitimacy. The implication of the legitimacy cost of terrorism is that how rebel groups support their rebellion has important repercussions on the strategic calculus of using lethal terrorist violence against non-combatants versus using more conventional types of violence against state coercive apparatuses. The second chapter characterizes internal and external financing sources based on the common conception in existing literature and provides a broad picture of the trends of rebels' external financing sources over time and across groups. Although most rebel groups possess only one type of external financing source, many rebel organizations derive their available resources from a mixture of various external sources. The prominence of different external financing sources has also varied over time: after the end of the Cold War, there was a downward trend in the portion of conflicts with natural resources and external state supporters as a financing mechanism for rebel groups and an upward trend of financing from external non-state actors. This trend suggests that comprehensively understanding the relationship between external financing and rebels' use of deadly terrorist violence requires studying the disaggregated effect of different sources of external financing, the role of financing diversity, and the role of specific types of external non-state supporters.

Chapter 3 of the book delves into the role-specific external financing sources and external financing sources diversity. I posit that the importance of the legitimacy costs of terrorism for rebel groups varies comparatively, depending on the involvement of the local population in providing external financing to rebels. The chapter subsequently explores the implications of this comparative framework for rebel organizations with different sources of external financing and more diverse types of external financing. Chapter 4 explores the impact of support from external non-state actors and proposes that these actors seek to exert influence over the lethality of rebels' terrorist violence based on their own specific objectives and interests. The chapter subsequently examines the implications for the use of lethal terrorist violence, considering the varying motivations driving support from external rebel groups, diaspora groups, and NGOs. Chapter 5 formalizes the study's hypotheses, describes the research design, and presents the findings of the empirical analysis. The last chapter draws on the proposed theoretical mechanisms, qualitative evidence, and empirical findings to examine the implications of this book on counterinsurgency endeavours that prioritize the safeguarding of civilians.

1 Benefits and Costs of Terrorism versus Conventional Warfare

In this chapter, terrorism is defined as the premeditated use of violence by non-state groups against non-combatant targets in order to achieve a political goal through the intimidation of a wider audience beyond the immediate victims (Enders and Sandler 2011). Although the surge in global terrorist attacks appears to reflect an increasing use of this form of violence in increasingly complex and internationalized civil wars, not all rebel groups use terrorism in civil wars (Clauset and Gleditsch 2012; Findley and Young 2012). Furthermore, the degree to which rebels deliberately target non-combatants with terrorist violence as a complement to other more conventional warfare activities against state coercive apparatuses varies from rebel group to rebel group and for specific rebel groups over time (Belgioioso 2018; Fortna et al. 2018; Polo and Gleditsch 2016; Polo and González 2020; Stanton 2013). To comprehend the variability in the severity of terrorist violence that rebel groups utilize in civil wars, I employ a sociological framework that allows to conceptualize terrorist attacks and other forms of political violence including violent attacks against state coercive apparatuses as part of a unique coherent set of behaviours: the set of contentious politics. According to Tilly and Tarrow (2015), contentious politics comprises all behaviours that involve contention, collective actions, and politics. Contention, in this context, refers to making claims that bear on the interests of others, while collective action involves coordinating efforts done on behalf of a shared interest among actors. Politics pertains to interactions with decision-making entities and organizations that have an impact on rights and regulations. All extra-institutional violent and

DOI: 10.4324/9781003377139-2

non-violent actions that rebel groups might adopt to produce their desired political outcomes are subsumed within the definition of contentious political behaviours. After having identified terrorist attacks and other conventional forms of warfare activities as contentious political behaviours that rebels might adopt, I endeavour to identify the distinct characteristics of these two contentious political behaviours that may influence a rebel group's decision to adopt one form of violence over another. To this end, I draw upon the Rationalist Explanations of War as posited by Fearon in 1995, which aims to elucidate the onset of interstate conflicts. Fearon (1995) argues that "war is costly and risky, so rational states should have incentives to locate a negotiated settlement that all would prefer to the gamble of war" (380). Although all contentious political behaviours come with costs and risks, these factors are not uniform across different forms of such behaviours. Therefore, to fully understand the differences in the severity of terrorist violence employed by rebel groups in civil wars, it is essential to identify why dissident groups cannot opt for conventional violent methods against a state's coercive apparatuses alternative to the use of terrorist violence against civilians. To this end, this chapter conducts an investigation of the tactical benefits of targeting non-combatants through terrorist attacks versus using military violence to target state coercive apparatuses directly. Subsequently, the chapter delves into the risks involved in deliberately targeting non-combatants with terrorism, including the potential alienation of rebel groups' various audiences and the associated costs in terms of popular support and legitimacy.

Given these premises, one of the fundamental assumptions of this study is that leaders of rebel groups make rational decisions regarding the extent of terrorism-related violence they employ in civil wars by considering the costs and benefits associated with terrorism, as well as accounting for the financial needs of their organization. Existing accounts suggest that this is because terrorism offers specific benefits and costs that differ from those of more conventional military actions directed at state coercive apparatuses. Unlike conventional warfare activities involving the use of direct armed force between two parties, at least one of which is the government of a state, terrorist attacks do not aim to destroy or harm the opponent state militarily. While conventional warfare relies on brute force to achieve the rebels' objectives without requiring any significant decision-making on the part of the enemy, terrorism is primarily a coercive strategy. With terrorist violence, rebels aim to persuade the enemy or the population to give them what they want by threatening harm if they do not comply (Biddle and Friedman 2008; Schelling 2009). The benefits associated with terrorist attacks are linked to the tactical advantages of targeting civilians covertly, as opposed to openly targeting state coercive apparatuses.

Terrorism is a less costly military option in comparison to conventional warfare activities for several reasons. Firstly, conventional activities like guerrilla attacks and pitched battles directly expose rebels to high risks of death, injury, or imprisonment. Conversely, terrorism allows rebels to evade direct exposure to retaliatory violence from the state, lowering the cost of fighting while allowing them to progress towards their political objectives (Monlar et al. 1966). Secondly, terrorist activities require fewer fighters than normal warfare activities against states' militaries and do not necessitate the coordination of substantial numbers of troops (Bueno de Mesquita 2013). As such, terrorist attacks are less reliant on rebel groups' military proficiency, and even very small, poorly armed and trained rebel units can effectively carry out terrorist actions (Biddle and Friedman 2008; Record 2009). Thirdly, terrorist attacks rely on less costly military technology than conventional and guerrilla warfare (Gunaratna 2001, 1). Dispersed, low-tech terrorist attacks provide a tactical advantage by imposing costs while evading detection and elimination by superior armed forces (Beckett 2001; Buhaug et al. 2009; Cunningham 2010; Hultquist 2013). Notably, the specific nature of terrorist violence makes the coercive benefits of this type of violence tactically and strategically distinct from other forms of one-sided violence against civilians, such as mass killing and genocidal acts (Eck and Hultman 2007). These types of civilian victimization may have benefits and costs different from terrorist violence, placing them outside of the scope of this book.

Deliberately targeting non-combatants with terrorist violence, however, carries the risk of alienating the audiences of rebel groups, and therefore, it might imply significant costs in terms of local legitimacy and popular support. As Fortna et al. (2018) point out: "terrorist attacks that kill members of the population on whose behalf the group ostensibly fights will be the costliest in terms of popular support" (784). However, terrorist attacks that selectively target non-combatants within communities opposed by rebel groups can also estrange potential supporters. In fact, terrorist violence is widely regarded as a morally reprehensible form of aggression, as it entails the deliberate slaughter of non-combatants, including women and children. These groups are often viewed as non-threatening and deserving of protection, even in the midst of civil conflicts (see for e.g., Sjoberg 2013; Sjoberg and Peet 2011). Potential supporters may develop concerns that rebel groups that employ terrorist violence against civilians belonging to the communities that they oppose are more inclined to coerce and instrumentally target civilians to achieve their political objectives. In addition to moral objections to targeting civilians, potential supporters may also fear becoming victims of indiscriminate terrorist attacks, unless they are geographically separated from communities opposed by the rebel groups (Fortna et al. 2018). Moreover, potential supporters may worry that terrorism could lead to a hardening of the opponent state's positions, both in terms of retaliatory repressive actions and in negotiations. Terrorism is often used by rebels as a tactic of provocation aiming to make the opponent state respond by imposing indiscriminate repression on the local population and is known to harden the bargaining position of governments regarding acceptable agreements (Fortna 2015; de Mesquita and Dickson 2007; Walsh and Piazza 2010). Lastly, engaging in terrorist attacks against non-combatants can be viewed as counterproductive since it can undermine the legitimacy of the broader opposition's political cause both domestically and internationally (Chenoweth and Schock 2015).

The manner in which rebel groups sustain their rebellion has significant implications for the perceived importance of the legitimacy costs related to deadly terrorist acts targeting non-combatants. As rebel groups' survival and ability to wage war rely on their capacity to access financing, the potential legitimacy costs associated with terrorist attacks against civilians became more salient for rebels to the extent that groups' financing strategies depend on the collaboration of the local population. The greater the risk of being unable to sustain a military campaign by losing access to financing sources, the less appealing it becomes for rebel groups to employ terrorist violence against civilians, even though it may offer benefits compared to conventional military violence.

Rebel groups, however, have several potential avenues to secure the financing necessary to support their rebellions. They may secure resources 'internally' through the support of local populations or 'externally' through the support of foreign states, external non-state organizations, and the exploitation of natural resources (Collier et al. 1999). Crucially, as we will see in Chapter 2, the sources of financing vary across rebel groups and over time, and globally the prevalence of financing sources has also changed since the end of the Cold War. Chapter 2 will delve into these two broad trends in greater depth, examining the empirical puzzle that motivates the book's emphasis on analysing the disaggregated impact of diverse external financing sources, the role of financing sources diversity, and the role of distinct non-state external supporters.

2 Empirical Trends of External Financing

In this book, the terms 'internal' and 'external' financing sources for rebel groups in civil conflicts are used according to the conceptualization in established scholarly works. Specifically, rebel groups may sustain their armed campaigns by securing resources through local popular support (i.e., 'internal' financing), or alternatively, by obtaining financing 'externally' through the exploitation of natural resources, the support of foreign states, and the support of external non-state organizations (Collier et al. 1999). Chapter 3 will provide a detailed discussion of how the long-term exploitation of natural resources, traditionally categorized as an 'external' financing method, is usually tightly dependent on the active compliance of the local population with the will and agenda of rebel groups. The aim of this chapter, instead, is to systematize existing evidence on the trends of rebels' external financing – according to the established conceptualization – globally over time and across groups. The broad picture of the empirical tendencies regarding external financing methods available to rebels in civil wars, exemplified below, motivates this book's empirical investigation. This picture underscores the importance of a more nuanced understanding of the effects of different sources of external financing, external financing diversity, and external financing provided by different non-state actors for the portfolio of killings of rebel groups in contemporary insurgencies.

The quantitative literature on rebel groups' financing sources in civil wars has grown substantially over the last two decades. These works have focused both on the driving motives of external support to far-away armed rebellions and the effects that external

DOI: 10.4324/9781003377139-3

financing has on various civil wars dynamics and outcomes. For example, external states' support to warring parties has been found to affect civil wars onsets (Cunningham 2016; Regan and Meachum 2014), duration (N. Anderson 2019; Aydin and Regan 2012; Cunningham 2010; Roberts 2019; Testerman 2015), spill over to interstate disputes (Schultz 2010), termination (Jones 2017; Keels et al. 2021; Lyall and Wilson 2009; Sawyer et al. 2017), recurrence (Karlén 2017), democratization (Colaresi 2014), civilian abuse (Salehyan et al. 2014), and sexual violence (Johansson and Sarwari 2019). Existing quantitative works have also extensively explored the link between natural resource exploitation and civil wars' dynamics and outcomes. While country-level studies find mixed results between primary commodity exports and civil war (Basedau and Lay 2009; Koubi et al. 2014; Ross 2004), subnational studies find that natural resources are associated with higher levels of conflict using some specifications, though the results vary widely by data source and world region (Denly et al. 2022), and that the availability of natural resources affects the temporal variation of civil war violence intensity (Hinkkainen Elliott and Kreutz 2019), the duration of the violent conflict (Berman et al. 2017; Lujala 2009), and the occurrence of terrorist attacks (Fortna et al. 2018).

The datasets utilized in these studies are not suitable for directly analysing the comparative impact of various external financing sources or external financing sources' diversity on the lethality of terrorist violence in civil war. Nor can they be used to investigate the effect of different types of external non-state supporters. This is because existing datasets are limited to either foreign state supporters or exploitation/presence of natural resources individually or only contain information on foreign states and external rebel groups. Other datasets merely provide measures of the type of external financing available to rebel groups aggregated across various external sources of financing. However, existing studies and datasets, taken together, provide a wealth of information on external sources of financing for rebel groups. This information can be utilized to gain a comprehensive understanding of various temporal trends. The present chapter endeavours to triangulate empirical observations on external financing sources in existing works by examining the descriptive evidence reported in various quantitative and qualitative studies on external supporters and natural resource exploitation. Through this analysis, I aim to construct a coherent view of the phenomenon of rebel groups' external financing over time.

The use of external financing by rebel organizations during civil conflicts is far from the deviation to the norm (Meier et al. 2022). Fortna et al. (2018) demonstrate that 61% of the rebel organizations in their study between 1970 and 2007 received some form of support from various external sources. However, Fortna et al. (2018) aggregate instances of financing provided by foreign states, external rebel groups, and other non-state actors. Meier et al. (2022) reveal a more nuanced picture of rebel groups' sources of external support, indicating that external backing from both foreign states and external rebel organizations has become more prevalent in armed conflicts. Crucially, the number of external states and non-state armed actors involved in financing armed groups in civil wars has increased exponentially since the beginning of the 21st century (Meier et al. 2022). When natural resource exploitation by rebel groups is factored in as an external source of financing, the percentage of externally financed insurgencies increased to 86% of the rebel organizations in the sample of Fortna et al. (2018). This evidence implies that only a (large) minority of rebel organizations rely exclusively on the direct support of the local population to finance their armed campaigns.

Existing empirical works also suggest that rebel groups' external financing sources have varied significantly over time. Existing quantitative evidence concurs on the pivotal and constant role played by foreign states in providing support to rebel groups and states involved in civil wars over time. In the UCDP External Support Dataset (ESD), the largest share (89%) of external support to states and non-states warring parties in civil wars comes from foreign state supporters (Meier et al. 2022). Similarly, Byman et al. (2001) find that out of 74 post-Cold War rebel organizations observed between 1991 and 2000, 44 were supported by foreign states. However, existing empirical evidence suggests that there has been a substantial shift in the nature of the sources of external financing for rebel groups since the end of the Cold War, with external non-state groups such as diaspora organizations, foreign NGOs, and external rebel movements gaining a prominent role in fostering and sustaining the campaigns of rebel organizations (Byman et al. 2001; Collier et al. 1999; Meier et al. 2022). Moghadam and Wyss (2020) note that armed non-state actors have in recent years adopted financing roles similar to those traditionally held by foreign states (120). Meier et al. (2022) also provide evidence that the number of rebel groups providing external support to warring parties has increased since the end of the Cold War. They note that

> [w]hile (...) the PLO, UNITA, and ELF (...) [were] the only rebel organization supporters active in 1975, the number of external rebel organizations supporting warring partied peaked in 2012 with 38 rebel groups providing external support, such as Al-Shabaab training Boko Haram combatants, and it has stayed above a count of 20 ever since.
>
> (6)

According to Baser and Swain (2008), in the post-Cold War era marked by globalization, diaspora communities have also emerged as crucial sponsors of rebel groups. This can be attributed to their comparatively greater economic resources compared to their home countries, along with their enhanced lobbying capability and greater freedom of expression.

In contrast to the increased prominence of non-state supporters, existing empirical evidence suggests a decrease in the use of natural resources as an external source of financing for rebel organizations after the end of the Cold War. Using a sample of 167 conflicts from the UCDP/PRIO Armed Conflict Dataset version 4-2007 (Harbom et al. 2008), Rustard and Binningsbø (2012) code internal armed conflicts between 1946 and 2006 based on the presence of natural resource–conflict links. They provide evidence that from the mid-1990s, "there is a downward trend in the fraction of conflicts with [natural resources as a] financing mechanisms [for rebel groups]" (538). In the 2000s, the relative number of natural resource conflicts dropped below 50%, and less than 15% of rebel organizations involved in these civil wars sustained their fight through the exploitation of natural resources (ibid.). In absolute terms, only 25% of the rebel organizations in the sample of Fortna et al. (2018) derived their financing from natural resources exploitation, and of this 25%, only 9% support their fight exclusively through the exploitation of natural resources. This suggests that the exploitation of natural resources did not become an important financing source after the end of the Cold War, as some observers expected (Ross 2004), and that the exploitation of natural resources is currently a less prominent method of external financing for rebel groups in civil wars.

Existing empirical evidence also demonstrates that a large minority of dissident organizations obtain financing for their campaigns from a combination of external sources. However, the current empirical evidence available on external financing diversity is limited to aggregated measures of external supporters and natural resources. In particular, in Fortna et al. (2018), 16% of rebel organizations observed from 1970 to 2007 obtained financing through a combination of natural resources exploitation and external actors. In my sample from 1989 to 2009, the percentage of rebel organizations using at least two sources of external financing (including foreign state actors, external rebel organizations, diaspora groups and NGOs, and natural resources) is approximately 20%. Given that the number of external states and non-state armed actors involved in financing armed groups in civil wars has increased exponentially since the end of the Cold War and that diaspora and NGOs are also gaining prominence as supporters of rebel organizations, knowledge on the correlation of the external financing sources diversity and rebels' contentious political behaviours is increasingly salient to shape current – and possibly future – counter-insurgency operations.

In summary, while most rebel groups rely on external financing to fund their campaigns, the prominence of various external financing sources has changed over time. Evidence shows a decline in conflicts where natural resources are used as a financing mechanism for rebel groups since the end of the Cold War. Currently, natural resource exploitation is the least common source of financing compared to support from foreign states and external non-state actors. On the other hand, external financing from non-state actors, such as diasporas and NGOs, and external rebel groups is becoming increasingly prominent in sustaining the campaigns of far-away rebel organizations. While the majority of rebel groups use only one type of external financing source, a significant and increasing minority obtain financing from a mixture of various external sources. Considering the relevance of these patterns for present programmes directed towards protecting populations from human rights violations and crimes against humanity during civil wars, I shall investigate the relative influence of particular financing sources and the range of external financing on the severity of terrorism in civil wars in Chapter 3. Subsequently, in Chapter 4, I will explore the impact of different external non-state supporters on the lethality of terrorist violence.

3 External Financing and the Lethality of Terrorism

Understanding the relative importance of specific external financing sources available to rebel groups and the role of financing sources diversity for the lethality of terrorism in civil wars can help inform policy discussions and improve decisions to address human rights abuses in civil war settings. This is because the prominence of external financing sources used by rebel organizations has changed over time, with a growing number of organizations relying on a mixture of external financing sources to sustain their armed campaigns. However, the current literature suffers from a lack of comprehensive scientific knowledge regarding the relative impacts of different external financing sources and financing sources' diversity on the lethality of terrorist violence in civil wars. In fact, the effects of these financing methods on the dynamics of civil war violence have primarily been studied in isolation rather than in comparative terms or in consideration of their contemporaneous occurrence. The failure to account for the full empirical variation of external financing sources may bias the findings of current analyses on external financing and civil war violence. This is concerning as the vast majority of the literature on this topic assumes that rebel groups' decisions regarding the use of terrorist violence depend on the ways in which financing impacts the decision of using terrorism. In this chapter, I argue that, for rebel groups, the importance of the legitimacy costs of terrorist violence varies depending on the role that the local population plays in making financing available to them. This chapter will explore the implications of this argument for each type of external financing source potentially available to rebel groups in comparison with

DOI: 10.4324/9781003377139-4

each other (Section 3.1), as well as for external financing source diversity (Section 3.2).

I assume that the way in which rebel groups finance their rebellion has significant consequences on the importance of legitimacy costs associated with using lethal terrorist violence against civilians. Since the ability to access economic profits and military resources is fundamental to the survival and prosecution of war by rebel groups, any contentious political behaviour that endangers the availability of financing in the short or long term is likely to be considered as an ineffective way to advance their goals. Thus, even though targeting civilians with terrorist violence might provide tactical advantages over using conventional warfare against state coercive apparatuses, the costs associated with alienating local supporters are likely to motivate rebel groups to restrain from employing lethal terrorist attacks to the extent that their financing availability depends on the local population.

Empirical studies support the notion that the lethality of terrorist attacks is a strategic calculation made by dissident organizations. Rebel groups carefully consider the expected number of casualties when planning terrorist attacks, as highly lethal attacks against civilian targets risk alienating their constituencies and causing loss of support (Valentino et al. 2004). For example, Davis (2013, 287) notes that female suicide bombers were systematically deployed in Iraq with the specific aim of creating a large number of casualties. The empirical findings of Polo and Gleditsch (2016) and Stanton (2013) also support this notion. Their works examine the costs and benefits of highly lethal terrorist campaigns and the strategic decision-making of dissident organizations in civil wars to target specific objectives with terrorist violence. The studies show that rebel groups with objectives and ideologies that can appeal to a broader audience are less inclined to carry out terrorist attacks resulting in a high number of civilian casualties, and they are more likely to target buildings or infrastructure with lower-casualty rates. These results also suggest that for rebel groups striving to gain local support or whose survival depends on the benevolence of the local population, highly lethal terrorist attacks may not be an effective means to achieve political and military objectives.

The use of terrorist attacks with high casualties in contested areas of civil war may result in not only a loss of popular legitimacy but also in active resistance by local civilians against the rebels. Despite being commonly seen as passive actors, the literature on rebel governance shows that local populations in contested areas of civil wars can have a significant impact on rebel groups' ability to survive and continue their fight (see for e.g., Arjona 2016; Rubin 2020). The local populous can play an active role to shape the fortune of rebel groups: they can provide financial, military, and logistics assistance to sustain their campaigns, ignore their orders and withdraw compliance, flee from violence and contested territories (Hancock and Mitchell 2007), resist them through non-violent or violent methods (Dasgupta 2012; Jentzsch Corinna 2014; Kaplan 2013; Schubiger 2021), or even assist government forces in their counter-insurgency efforts (Kalyvas 2006). As a result, rebel groups aiming to control a territory and its population are motivated to become stationary (Olson 1993), minimize harm to civilians (Stanton 2013), and use governing strategies that generate voluntary compliance for resource extraction (Levi 1989).

Therefore, studies on rebel governance suggest that groups relying on local populations as their primary source of financing have specific incentives to cultivate collaborative relationships with them. This literature also suggests that insurgents that depend on internal financing do not only have incentives from refraining from using violent coercion against civilians, but they also have incentives to establish order and provide security, services, and goods to the population in contested areas. This is necessary to ensure a stable flow of internal financing that is crucial for their organizational survival and armed campaigns. The Farabundo Martí National Liberation Front's (FMLN) violent campaign against the Salvadorian government is an example of this. Observers have noted that the FMLN's ability to wage war and survive as an organization was closely tied to the availability of internal financing and voluntary support from the local population in contested areas. "Despite the high risk of insurgent activism, support by many (…) poor rural residents were an essential element of the FMLN's military and political capacity throughout the war, according to a wide range of analyses, including that of the U.S. military officers" (Viterna 2014, 10). To ensure a temporally sustained availability of internal financing, the FML implemented a governing strategy based on the provision of key services instead of the violent coercion of the local population. In the Guazapa Volcano area of El Salvador, the local civilians saw their economic and political lives increasingly interdependent with the FMLN, via their provision of food, education, and security. These policies contributed to the FMLN's ability to obtain internal financing through the influx of financial and military resources from one-third of the local population over the entire duration of the civil war, in addition to the fixed contribution required from individuals to remain in the contested areas (Wickham-Crowley 2015; Wood 2003).

Given the significant legitimacy costs associated with civilian casualties resulting from terrorist attacks, I assume that insurgent groups relying solely on local populations for financial support in civil wars are overall not inclined to engage in highly lethal terrorist violence. This raises an important question about the implications for rebel organizations that employ other common financing methods, such as natural resource exploitation, support from foreign states, and external non-state organizations. The effects of these external financing methods on the lethality of terrorist violence are also likely to depend on the extent to which the local population affect the availability of the financing sources. I expect that this varies significantly across external financing sources. I claim that reliance on external financing from foreign states and non-state organizations, compared to natural resources, reduces the impact of local legitimacy costs associated with targeting non-combatants in terrorist attacks. This leads rebel groups with external financing from foreign states and non-state organizations to carry out more lethal terrorist attacks in civil war contexts. Additionally, I claim that the access to more diverse external sources of financing decreases the impact of local legitimacy costs associated with terrorism and that, in turn, this leads rebel groups to perpetrate more intense terrorist violence. In the remaining of this chapter, I will justify in detail the theoretical claims outlined above and discuss three case studies that provide initial qualitative and illustrative support for my theoretical expectations.

3.1 Different External Financing, Different Legitimacy Costs

As the salience of the cost on legitimacy associated with terrorism decreases due to reduced dependence on the local population for financing, terrorist violence becomes a more cost-effective method of political contention for rebel groups in civil wars. Existing literature has demonstrated that foreign state support to rebel groups engaged in civil war violence increases the likelihood of civilians becoming victims of rebels' violence. This is because financing from foreign states reduces rebel groups' reliance on the local population in contested areas to obtain the necessary resources for survival. Consequently, rebels are less incentivized to win the hearts and minds of local civilians and use more coercion to achieve their objectives. I claim that rebel groups reliant on external non-state groups for financing are similarly unrestricted in their use of lethal terrorist violence against non-combatants, compared to groups reliant on foreign states. This is because, while rebel groups risk alienating foreign and external non-state sponsors through terrorist violence, these risks are likely to be weaker than those of alienating the local population. Firstly, external actors do not bear direct costs for terrorist violence. Secondly, external non-state groups are not subject to direct retaliatory repression by the warring state as a result of terrorist violence. Thirdly, it is more difficult for external audiences to distinguish between deliberate targeting of non-combatants and instances of 'collateral damage'. Lastly, concerns of external supporters over the intensity of terrorist violence perpetrated by their rebel allies vary significantly depending on their specific interests (see Salehyan et al. 2014; Chapter 4). Therefore, reliance on any external actors for financing reduces the impact of legitimacy costs associated with killing local civilians in terrorist campaigns and leads rebel groups to perpetrate more intense terrorist killings compared to financing obtained from or through local popular supporters.

Rebel groups that rely on external financing from natural resource exploitation, on the contrary, face higher local legitimacy costs than rebels who obtain financing from any type of external actor. Therefore, they are more likely to refrain from intense civilian killings with terrorist violence. Unlike the resources provided by external supporters, natural resource exploitation typically produces rents that are location specific (Collier and Hoeffler 1999). This implies that for rebel groups to fully exploit financing from natural resources, they need to have some level of local stability, control over natural resource extraction, and/or possibly long-term compliance from the local population. Instability and violence tend to limit the economic profitability of natural resources (Hinkkainen Elliott and Kreutz 2019; Keen 1998). Higher levels of violent confrontation over natural resources, in fact, lead to a decreased revenue and subsequently fewer financing available for rebels to sustain their fight and organization. In line with this idea, various empirical works have noted that in highly contested natural resources-rich areas it is not uncommon for opponent warring parties to stop fighting and cooperate in order to optimize the extraction of natural resources (Lujala 2009; Ross 2004; Snyder 2006). Ross (2004), for example, finds that in 88% of civil conflicts fought over resources, opponents intermittently collaborate with each other in exploiting the same natural resource they fight over, entering "a kind of commercial equilibrium" (56). For example, in Angola, UNITA (the National Union for the Total Independence of Angola) rebels and state military avoided direct violent confrontations to sift diamonds on opposite banks of the Cuango Valley's river (Billon 2013).

The extraction, cultivation, refinement, transportation, and distribution of natural resources rely also on the compliance of the local civilian population, either indirectly as enablers or directly as labourers. For instance, the Revolutionary United Front (RUF) in Sierra Leone managed to finance its rebellion for a period through the exploitation of diamond fields by employing a large number of civilian workers to sift the precious gems (Salehyan et al. 2014; Vorrath 2014). Similarly, for oil to become a profitable source of financing, rebel groups must employ specialized labour forces and develop industrial capacities to manage its extraction, refinement, and commercialization (Schultze-Kraft 2017; Steenkamp 2017). The fruition of drug crops, such as the Coca plant in Colombia, opium in Afghanistan and Myanmar, or cannabis in West Africa, requires a specialized and labour-intensive process, necessitating rebels to employ a significant number of local labourers to realize any financial benefit (Goodhand 2008; Skaperdas 2008; Steenkamp 2017; Vorrath 2014).

Rebels cannot use coercion to sustainably finance their organizations through natural resource exploitation because this requires at least some level of compliance and/or collaboration of the local population. If civilians resist rebels' violent coercion, attempt to flee contested areas, or deny cooperation, the rebel groups' capacity to survive and wage war can be severely diminished. For instance, Lidow (2016) finds that farmers in Liberia refused to clear their lands, fearing their products would be looted by rebels during the upcoming farming season, as a means to extort pressure on rebels and avoid coercive violence. Therefore, rebel groups that seek long-term collaborative relationships with locals on natural resource extraction and commercialization are more likely to restrain from using terrorist violence against civilians than those depending on external actors for financing. Such rebel groups are more likely to aim to gain legitimacy as governing agencies by providing goods and services to the population in conflict-affected areas.

Next, I discuss two case studies that exemplify the theoretical mechanisms discussed so far. In the first case, I illustrate how a change in financing sources for the United Liberation Front of Assam (ULFA), from internal local supporters to external states and non-state actors, incentivized the ULFA to increase the lethality of their terrorist violence against the Assamese population, whom they aimed to represent and protect against the abuses of the Central Indian State. In the second case, I demonstrate how the external financing strategy the Karen National Union (KNU), primarily based on the extraction and commercialization of natural resources within contested areas, led the KNU to consistently restrain from the use of intense terrorist violence against civilians in the contested territories. As expected, the KNU's use of natural resources as a source of financing motivated the establishment of a sophisticated governance system that embedded the rebels in the local population.

Case 1. The United Liberation Front of Assam (ULFA)

The ULFA was formed in 1979, by a group of Assamese youths that wanted to mount an armed struggle against the Indian government to end 'Indian colonialism' and create an independent state of Assam. At its outset, with the political agenda of 'unity, revolution, and liberation' (Saikia 2012), the ULFA youths represented a radical faction of the Assam Movement, one of the most powerful non-violent civil resistance campaigns in India post-independence, whose main goals were to safeguard the interests and identity of the indigenous population of Assam by promoting the local economy and deporting Bangladeshi illegal immigrants (Dasgupta 2012, 120). In 1985, the signing of the Assam Accord with the Indian government, and the striking election victory of the Asom Gana Parishad (AGP), a newly constituted party that was the direct expression of the Assam Movement leadership, ended the popular non-violent mobilization in the state of Assam. However, the ULFA gained popularity within the first and second terms of the AGP in the government, as it became increasingly clear to the local population and to former Assam Movement activists that the AGP leadership was unable to fulfil their promises of political change and enforce the terms of the Assam Accord.

The ULFA exploited the political vacuum opened up by the AGP in government and captured the support of disillusioned Assamese by building new roads, cracking down on public littering, honouring local artists and writers, policing neighbourhoods, and enforcing bans on the sale and consumption of alcoholic drinks (Dasgupta 2012; Gohain 2007). Because of these initiatives, the members of the ULFA were described as 'idealistic and patriotic youths' by local newspapers (Gohain 2007, 1012) and "[m]any (Assamese citizens) welcomed their sabre-rattling as a sound way to put the enemy of Assam in their places" (ibid.). However, the ULFA's supporters were not limited to the local population and to the news outlets but extended to the local government, bureaucracy, and police. In fact, expecting to use the ULFA as a means to intimidate political rivals, the AGP-governed local authorities "took a rather indulgent view on their activities" (ibid.) and they provided the UFLA with an access to money and safe haven. The fact that ULFA headquarters was very close to major local government administrative offices in the far eastern corner of Assam and that locals refused to disclose the ULFA's whereabouts to Indian authorities indicate the active local support that ULFA enjoyed from the government and the Assamese population in the first phase of its activity (Gohain 2007; Sanjoy 1995).

This local support allowed the ULFA to acquire a substantial amount of financing through extortions and ransoms targeted at managers and superintendents of 'foreign-owned' rich tea plantations. "The story goes that a huge amount of money changed hands as big traders from outside bought security [from the ULFA] in a situation where the police appeared demoralized" (Gohain 2007, 1015). However, the ULFA's financing strategy had to change at the beginning of the 90s, when various powerful tea lobby groups in London persuaded the Indian central government – through the High Indian Commission – to start a full-scale counter-insurgency operation in Assam to stop the ULFA and its 'campaign of intimidation and extortion'. The local Assamese government and its bureaucratic structure had to comply with the Indian central government and collaborate in the counter-insurgency efforts to ensure their survival. ULFA's leaders and fighters that survived the Indian crackdown, who did not surrender or were co-opted, had to find new external financing sources. After the crackdown, a number of external supporters across the Assamese border in Bhutan, Myanmar, and Bangladesh started to provide financing to the ULFA's remaining active cadres. Abroad, the ULFA received shelter, military training, arms, and money from, among others, the Bhutanese government, the Bangladesh Rifles, the Pakistani Inter-Service Intelligence, the Chin National Liberation Army, the Liberation Tigers of Tamil Eelam, and the Nepalese Maoist (Dasgupta 2012; Gohain 2007; Kumar 2004). As a result of this external financing, the ULFA quickly (re-)built a sizable armed organization and started a low-intensity war against the Indian government.

Despite its increased military power and organizational capability, soon after the shift of financing provision from internal to external, the ULFA substantially increased the intensity of terrorist violence against Assamese civilians (Dasgupta 2012; Gohain 2007). This trend increased over time as the organization and its leadership became progressively more dependent on external supporters for financing. Data provided by the Delhi-based Institute of Conflict Management show, for example, that after the first counter-insurgency, between 1998 and 2000 the violence used by the ULFA was mostly aimed at Assamese civilians to terrorize them and/or forcibly raise funds. This irregular violence included murder/attack/assault, lootings/extortion, explosions, kidnappings, and arson besides regular attacks on police/security forces (Dasgupta 2012, 123). According to my data drawing on the Global Terrorist Database (START 2022) and the UCDP Conflict Database (Högbladh et al. 2011), the ULFA killed yearly on average more Assamese civilians than Indian military personnel between the years 1990 and 2009. In total, the Global Terrorist Database reports that the ULFA was responsible for more than

600 civilian deaths in terrorist attacks over their 8 years of civil war against the Central Indian State.

Some argue that ULFA increased its terrorist killings because the group lost popularity due to changing its position on the issue of illegal immigration from Bangladesh, thus moving away from the original political goal of the Assamese Movement (Dasgupta 2012). However, this claim is contradicted by local Assamese academics who assert that the nationalist movement did not materialize out of specific, well-defined grievances and demands in the first place (Gohain 2007). It is more plausible that ULFA shifted to increasingly intense terrorist killings as a result of the change in financing sources from internal to external, following the first counter-insurgency operation carried out by the Central Indian Government military and the local Assamese government. The loss of internal financing and support from the local AGP administration and the population, and the acquisition of external financing from states and non-state actors decreased the salience of the local legitimacy costs of terrorism violence for the ULFA. From the 1990s, killing civilians with terrorism not only stopped having long-term consequences for ULFA's financing availability, but its cadres were also able to safely hide abroad and avoid direct retaliation from the Indian state coercive apparatus. This claim is supported by the success of counter-terrorist efforts carried out at the expense of ULFA in Bhutan, as evidence shows that the number of civilian killings in Assam decreased as ULFA cadres were stripped out of their foreign training camps and political connections (Kumar 2004).

As terrorist killings intensified in Assam, the local population took an active role in resisting the ULFA (Dasgupta 2012). Assamese people and civil society exerted political pressure on the Assamese state and the Indian central government to carry out various counter-insurgency operations. They engaged in nonviolent protests against the ULFA, condemned their violent activities, and demanded that they lay down their arms and engage in peaceful negotiations. Additionally, they provided valuable intelligence to the state and national security forces and policed their own areas, reporting any suspicious activities by the ULFA to the state authorities. Due to its declining popular support and various counter-insurgency operations, the ULFA is now substantially weakened (Kumar 2004).

Case 2. The Karen National Union (KNU)

The KNU was established in 1974 by Karen politicians, lawyers, civil servants, and other educated Karen nationalists, with the aim of advocating for greater autonomy for the Karen people in the context of Myanmar's independence from Great Britain. In the 1990s, the KNU launched a large-scale armed campaign to call for the establishment of a Federal Democratic Union of Myanmar, in which all citizens could be equal. The Karen ethnic group is the third-largest ethnic nationality in Myanmar. The term Karen refers to a fluid grouping of related ethnicities that have mutually unintelligible languages but are connected through customs, traditions, and a long history of shared communities. These ethnic groups inhabit the border regions of Myanmar and Thailand and are concentrated in the Ayeyarwady, Bago, and Yangon Regions. Because of the diverse composition of the Karen people, the KNU saw a federal system that provides ethnically designated states with internal autonomy, in addition to power-sharing arrangements at the central level, as its ultimate political objective. Its central grievance was, in fact, the absolute domination of the Myanmar state's structures by the Bamar ethnic group and its military leaders.

Since its foundation, the KNU has depended on financing from the exploitation of local natural resources. During the Cold War, the main source of financing for the KNU came from revenues connected to the production, taxation, and trade of opium (Woods 2018). However, in the 1990s, as a result of changing bilateral relations between Thailand and Myanmar and harsher measures on drug production and trafficking, the KNU turned to the extraction of other natural resources in the territories under its control (Brenner 2018). In this second phase, the primary sources of financing became the logging and mining sectors. Specifically, the KNU controlled local production in gold, tin, and antimony mines (Dudouet and Galvanek 2018; Jolliffe 2016; Woods 2018). The KNU's ability to successfully manage the mining sector and finance armed activities against the Myanmar state became evident as the largest artisanal industry in the Karen-populated territories post-Cold War was mining. In this period, local and migrant artisanal labourers seeking employment in KNU-controlled areas were typically informally organized or formally regulated directly by the KNU military structure, either as labourers or soldiers.

Apart from being integrated into the KNU bureaucratic machine, local civilian labourers working in logging and mining in the contested areas were taxed by the KNU. Although there is evidence of instances of coercive taxation, starting from the 90s, most people in the Karen regions supported the KNU voluntarily and were accustomed to paying taxes to them (Dudouet and Galvanek 2018). More recently, over the past ten years, the KNU has been able to adopt a more decentralized strategy to gather financing from the extraction of natural resources. Rather than directly organizing labourers through its bureaucratic and military structure, the KNU outsources mining concessions to local extraction companies owned by local Karen nationals. These companies are tasked with generating revenues for the rebel organization (Karen News 2012). This system might suggest the success of the KNU in gaining local legitimacy as a governing body. Interestingly, evidence shows how the opening, management, and closure of mining sites are heavily subjected to the preferences and feedback of the local population. Complaints from the local population that a mining site is polluting the environment, destroying livestock, and damaging plantations are followed by the closure of the site and the withdrawal of mining concessions from the extraction companies (ibid.). This exemplifies how important it is for the KNU to maintain the benevolence of the local population.

The revenues from logging and mining are collected locally and then funnelled up through the KNU hierarchy to be distributed among the seven districts under the rebel organization's administration. While KNU village leaders can keep 10% of the collected sums, most of the taxation and revenue goes to KNU fighters. Despite this well-established financing system, the KNU is relatively poor compared to other large rebel organizations in Myanmar, such as the Kachin Independence Organization and the United Wa State Party (Jolliffe 2016). However, since the financing of the KNU's armed campaigns has always been connected to the exploitation and extraction of natural resources, the group developed incentives to establish itself as a governance actor deeply embedded in local large rural communities, where the Myanmar state has failed to establish stable governance arrangements.

The longevity and strength of the KNU have come from close, peaceful relations with rural communities. Over the course of the war, the KNU has adopted a strong pro-human rights stance, positioning itself as a protector of the local population in response to the high level of human rights abuses carried out by the government. In the territories under its control, the KNU has set up and enforced a legitimate basic justice system with a police force and accessible registers. The KNU has also regulated and provided ownership titles for agricultural land, managed forestry and other forms of land use, and provided basic social services, including education and primary healthcare, in line with the preferences of the local Karen citizens. To gather support and legitimacy from the local Karen population, the KNU has established various community-based organizations with officially mandated roles in relation to the rebel structure that operates in its controlled areas. Some of these community-based organizations were directly connected to the exploitation and extraction of natural resources. For example, the Federation of Trade Unions–Kare, which included Karen agriculture workers, reports to the Organizing and Information Department and has rights and responsibilities in this sector as part of the KNU itself (Jolliffe 2016).

According to information reported in the Global Terrorist Database (START 2022), KNU's use of terrorist violence has been generally limited during the course of its armed campaign. Half of the attacks carried out by the group between 1990 and 2009 caused zero casualties, and almost 15% of the remaining attacks caused less than ten casualties. The low count of casualties is even more significant when considering KNU's advanced military capabilities. When terrorist attacks were used to kill civilians, these were highly discriminated attacks generally directed against non-local civilians or government collaborators. The vast majority of KNU's terrorist attacks targeted and killed government workers in contested territories, employees of private companies hired by the Myanmar government to provide services in the contested territories, and employees of private foreign companies engaging in business ventures related to the exploitation of local natural resources in KNU-controlled areas. KNUs' terrorist-related casualties amount to a total of 93 people killed between 1990 and 2009 in various attacks against the government and private companies. Of these, only 28 local Karen civilians appear to have died as a result of terrorist violence carried out by the KNU against transports or state-owned public buildings during the period of observation.

3.2 The Role of Diversity of External Financing Methods

For many rebel organizations, available financing derives from a mixture of various external sources. Fortna et al. (2018, 788) show, for example, that in 11% of the years observed in their study, rebel groups relied on a mixture of looting of natural resources and foreign states' support. In my sample, 17% of the observations correspond to years in which rebels relied on two external financing sources, while almost 2% of the observations correspond to years in which rebels rely on all three types of external resources simultaneously. The comparative legitimacy-cost theory proposed above suggests that rebels with support of foreign states or external non-state actors are overall less constrained in perpetrating terrorism killings, even when they can contemporaneously exploit natural resources or they are supported by the local population. This is because the presence of financing from any external actor makes the potential costs of alienating internal audiences less impactful on the capacity of rebel groups to survive and wage war. Moreover, the theory proposed above implies that rebels with more diverse sources of external financing are less constrained in perpetrating terrorism killings. This is because a higher diversification of external sources of financing is likely to make the potential costs of alienating any one audience (internal or external) less impactful on the overall capacity of rebel groups to survive and wage war.

As explained in Chapter 2, terrorist attacks against civilians are often preferred to other conventional warfare activities because they are militarily cheaper. Conventional warfare activities against state coercive apparatuses require large amounts of resources, such as personnel, equipment, and logistics, which are expensive to obtain and maintain. In contrast, terrorism relies on relatively inexpensive forms of lower-scale violence. Because terrorism is militarily cheaper than conventional warfare, it can be more accessible to groups that find themselves in a situation of military power imbalance fighting against state actors. However, even though terrorism may be militarily cheaper than conventional warfare, it comes with the risk of alienating supporters. Since multiple sources of external financing make rebel groups less dependent on any one of them, the salience of the legitimacy cost of terrorism decreases. In fact, the more diverse the external sources of financing, the easier it is for rebels to carry out acts of terrorism without fearing losing all the resources necessary to their survival. On the contrary, when rebel groups rely on fewer financing sources, the salience of the legitimacy cost of terrorism increases and can have consequences as bad as ceasing operations.

In other words, rebel groups that have access to a more diverse range of external financing sources are less restricted in their ability to carry out terrorist attacks because they are not as vulnerable to the consequences of alienating any one audience. As such, diversity of more external financing sources allows rebels to act more independently and use militarily cheaper violence such as terrorism to exert more pressure on their opponents to advance political goals without fearing consequences on their ability to survive as an organization. In contrast, rebel groups that rely on a fewer external financing sources are more vulnerable. If they carry out attacks that upsets their external supporter or the local individuals that allow them to extract and commercialize resources, they risk losing their financing. This can severely limit the ability to operate. The costs of alienating fewer available sources of financing are likely to be substantially higher.

Below, I present an illustrative case study that provides initial qualitative support for the mechanism discussed in this subsection. The case of the RUF in Sierra Leone shows how the group's reliance on diverse external sources for financing, including foreign states, external non-state actors, and natural resources, contributed to its use of highly lethal terrorist violence against civilians. In the long run, RUF's dependence on external actors for financing, coupled with the exploitation of natural resources, contributed to its incapacity to hold territory and extract natural resources sustainably.

Case 3. The Revolutionary United Front (RUF)

In 1991, a group of disaffected Sierra Leonean soldiers founded the RUF. The group waged a large-scale armed campaign against Sierra Leone until 2002 when it was militarily defeated. While the

RUF's ideology remains debated among scholars and experts, there is evidence that the group's initial political goal was to establish a new political system based on the distribution of wealth and power among the Sierra Leonean population (Erbrick 2012; Peters 2011; Richards 1998). Pan-Africanism and the belief that the government of Sierra Leone was dominated by Western interests and that foreign corporations exploited the country's resources influenced RUF's ideology at its emergence in the early 1990s (Abdullah 1998; Kruk 2020). The RUF's stated goal was to overthrow the government and establish a socialist system based on the principles of social justice, equality, and self-determination to redistribute the wealth and resources of the country more equitably among the population (Peters 2011; Richards 1998). The RUF also aimed at ending political corruption and economic mismanagement, which the group believed was preventing the majority of the population from benefiting from Sierra Leone's natural resources (Dudek 2021).

Despite its socialist ideology and its stated aims, from the early stages of the conflict with the Sierra Leonean government, the RUF gained a local reputation for its extensive use of brutal violence against the civilians it aimed to represent and protect (Mitton 2015). This violence included forcible recruitment, rape, and amputations as a means of terrorizing the people and coercing them into advancing its political goals. Allegedly, one of the main reasons that did not stop the RUF from restraining the use of terrorist attacks against the civilian population and other forms of civilian victimization was the group's reliance on diverse external sources for financing. The RUF's ability to survive and wage war, in fact, depended on financing provided by foreign states and external non-state actors, and on the financing obtained through the extraction and commercialization of natural resources. While the RUF's primary source of financing was the illicit trade in diamonds, which they could exploit as a financing method thanks to its control of key diamond-mining areas in Sierra Leone such as the Kono district, the group also received substantial support in the forms of arms, ammunition, and money in exchange for diamonds from Liberia's President Charles Taylor and other armed non-state actors in the region (Gberie 2005).

In the initial stages of the civil war, the RUF's dependence on diverse external sources of financing made the group less preoccupied with the local legitimacy costs derived from using terrorist violence against the population. In the long run, however, the RUF's dependence on external actors for financing, in addition to the exploitation of natural resources, contributed to its incapacity to hold territory and extract natural resources in a sustainable manner. The RUF failed to develop a stable base of support among the population in the contested areas because the resources provided by foreign states and external non-state actors as alternative sources of financing made the development of a coherent political program unnecessary (Truth and Reconciliation Commission of Sierra Leone 2004; Human Rights Watch 2005). The diversity of external financing methods available to the RUF also did not generate the incentives to establish the group as an accepted governance actor by local populations. Because of the intensity of violence against civilians, the group was unable to establish a stable and lasting base of operations, and its control over diamond mines and other natural resources was often short-lived (Richards 2002). In turn, this lack of control made it difficult for the RUF to sustain operations and incentivized the resort to use increasingly extreme forms of coercive violence against civilians to maintain financing availability after external supporters stopped financing the group (Malan et al. 2005).

Eventually, the RUF's use of brutal terrorist violence and failure to develop local support made it vulnerable to changes in regional politics and the shifting priorities of its external supporters (Gberie 2005). For example, under increasing international pressure in the late 1990s, Charles Taylor began to distance himself from the RUF and limit his military and financial support for the group (Human Rights Watch 2000; Malan et al. 2005). Having failed to develop local legitimacy, shifts in Taylor's support made the RUF substantially more vulnerable to counterinsurgency efforts by the Sierra Leonean government. The RUF's heavier reliance on external actors for financing also led to the group's inability to establish a stable and effective leadership structure, making it susceptible to infighting and competing interests and goals between different factions within the RUF (Abdullah 2007; Keen 1998; UN Security Council 2000). This lack of cohesion made it difficult for the RUF to effectively plan and execute their operations and contributed to the group's overall ineffectiveness. The group's use of terrorism against civilians, coupled with other forms of civilian victimization and its lack of a political agenda, made the RUF increasingly unpopular among the population, and it was eventually defeated by a combination of government forces and an UN-backed peacekeeping mission.

4 External Non-State Supporters and the Lethality of Terrorism

While Chapter 3 focuses on probing the relative effects of different types of external financing sources and the external financing sources diversity on the lethality of terrorist violence in civil wars, this chapter zooms in on the roles of different external non-state supporters. In particular, it aims to examine the role of external financing provided by the most common non-state supporters, namely external rebel groups, diasporas, and NGOs. A more comprehensive and systematic understanding of the ways in which specific external non-state supporters affect rebels' use of terrorist violence has important implications for informing the debates around modern counterinsurgency strategies. This is because since the end of the Cold War, external non-state actors such as diasporas, foreign NGOs, and external rebel organizations have played a prominent role in financing rebel groups Richards 2002) However, existing knowledge on the ways in which financing from external non-state actors affects rebels' use of lethal terrorist violence in civil wars remains limited, and existing academic works on this topic are characterized by a lack of systematic empirical investigations.

Existing quantitative research on the effect of external supporters on rebels' civilian victimization has mainly focused on examining and testing the effect of financing exerted by different types of foreign state actors, in line with the focus of more traditional Security Studies. With the exception of Petrova' s (2019) study on the relationship between diasporas' support for rebels and their adoption of non-violent civil resistance methods, no systematic work has been done on the relationship between the

DOI: 10.4324/9781003377139-5

support of external non-state actors and rebel groups' tactical choices. The vast majority of existing studies on the impacts of diaspora communities and NGOs on violent conflict dynamics are qualitative in nature and consist of case studies with contradictory narratives and findings. Only recently have more systematic data been developed on external non-state rebel group supporters (Meier et al. 2022), which have been employed to examine the drivers of support of external non-state armed actors in far-away conflicts. In summary, the role of external non-state sponsors in civil wars, although increasingly relevant, is acknowledged in only a small number of academic studies. As Moghadam and Whyss (2020) put it, "the causes, nature, and consequences of non-state sponsorship [to rebel groups] remain largely unexplored" (119).

As we delve into the role of specific types of external non-state actors, the theoretical premises of this chapter remain unchanged – the way in which rebel groups finance for their rebellion has significant implications for the legitimacy costs associated with the use of lethal terrorist violence against civilians. As outlined in Chapter 2, the risk of alienating the local population increases with the severity of terrorist campaigns, as civilians bear the brunt of the violence and subsequent retaliatory actions by the state. Local populations are also better able than external observers to distinguish between deliberate targeting of non-combatants with terrorist attacks and unintentional collateral damage. Thus, they are better equipped to identify when punishing rebel groups for abusive coercive behaviour is necessary. On average, reliance on any type of external actor for financing decreases the impact of the legitimacy costs associated with killing local civilians in terrorist campaigns. However, examining external non-state supporters in a disaggregated manner reveals that the salience of the costs of lethal terrorist violence can differ across different types of external non-state actors. Not only do rebel organizations face a greater risk of losing the support of some external non-state sponsors when using lethal terrorist violence, but some types of external non-state supporters may view lethal terrorism against civilians as a desirable contentious political behaviour.

In this chapter, I argue that external non-state actors assert influence over the lethality of terrorism used by rebels in civil wars based on their own objectives and interests. In other words, the impact of external non-state funders on the severity of terrorism perpetrated by rebel groups in civil wars varies depending on the goals of the specific non-state actor providing support to a particular rebel organization. The relationship between a rebel group and its external non-state supporters can be understood as a principal–agent relationship, with the external non-state supporter (the principal) providing financial, military, logistical, and/or political resources to the rebel group (the agent) in exchange for the group's cooperation and adherence to certain conditions or goals. In order to ensure alignment of interests and minimize the risk of the agent acting against the principal's interests, the principal screens potential agents and makes support conditional on the agent's behaviours. However, the relationship between external non-state support and rebel groups' terrorism is likely endogenous, as potential agents and principals anticipate each other's preferences and actions. External non-state supporters utilize screening mechanisms to identify rebel groups whose preferences align closely with their own and are more likely to support those rebels whose behaviour is in line with their preferences. Rebel groups receiving support from external non-state actors are more susceptible to sanctions and loss of support if their behaviours deviate from the preferences of their external sponsors. Consequently, rebel groups are more likely to conform to preferred behaviours of potential external non-state supporters before the support is deployed as a means to attract targeted external non-state supporters.

This chapter builds on existing research regarding the determinants of foreign state support for rebel groups, specifically investigating the relationship between regime type of foreign state supporters and rebel groups' use of civilian victimization. Previous literature has demonstrated that this relationship is influenced by the principal–agent dynamics between the sponsoring foreign state and the receiving rebel organization (Salehyan et al. 2014). Foreign states may sponsor rebel groups to achieve their geopolitical objectives, but this can create domestic and international risks for the sponsoring state. The theory suggests that regime type may influence the salience of these risks. For instance, democratic states may be more vulnerable to human rights lobbies and therefore more likely to have strong preferences regarding their protégées' behaviour towards civilians. Empirical evidence supports this idea, demonstrating that rebel groups supported by democratic states are less likely to engage in civilian victimization (Salehyan et al. 2014). This chapter expands on these findings by connecting existing research on the motives of external non-state actors' support for rebel groups with recent observations that armed non-state actors have taken on financing roles similar to those of states (Moghadam and Wyss 2020) and that diasporas and NGOs can impact conflict dynamics and rebel groups' contentious political behaviours (Petrova 2019; Roth 2015).

If one assumes that external non-state support affects the lethality of terrorism perpetrated by rebel groups depending on the external non-state supporter's objectives and interests, the first necessary step to comprehend these relationships is to investigate the motivations of different types of external non-state supporter. Existing qualitative work and small N empirical works suggest that the motivations of external rebel groups when supporting a rebellion are substantially different from those of foreign state actors, and that the motivation of diaspora communities and international NGOs also follow its own specific logic. Drawing on this literature, I argue that financing from diaspora communities and NGOs is likely to decrease the use of lethal terrorist violence against non-combatants because these organizations support rebel groups to minimize insecurity and shape favourable long-term political outcomes in conflict-affected areas (Byman et al. 2001; Petrova 2019). In contrast, external rebel group support is likely to increase the lethality of terrorist violence because rebel organizations support other armed groups to consolidate their international and domestic political influence (Moghadam and Wyss 2020) and view highly lethal terrorist attacks as a measure of the credible commitment of their rebel protégées (Hovil and Werker 2005). The rest of this chapter provides a detailed justification for these theoretical expectations and examines two case studies that offer initial illustrative support for my claims.

4.1 External Rebel Groups

Qualitative and small N comparative evidence suggests that external rebel groups provide support to other rebel organizations to advance their political influence (Byman et al. 2001; Moghadam and Wyss 2020). External armed groups view their rebel protégées as "political ancillaries" whose primary aim is to promote their political goals directly (Moghadam and Wyss 2020, 121). This motivation differs significantly from that of foreign state actors, who use rebel protégées as proxies to achieve their geopolitical military objectives. Moghadam and Whyss (2020) propose that the different motivations behind the support of foreign states and external rebel organizations to rebel organizations depend on differences in organizational capacities, status, and constraints. Foreign states are advanced bureaucratic machines, typically militarily superior to armed non-state actors, and they also enjoy domestic and international legitimacy over the territorial they control. While states may have interests in territories beyond their national borders, their survival as an organization generally does not depend on foreign military operations. On the contrary, states may face high international and domestic costs when participating directly in foreign military operations. To avoid these costs, foreign states use external rebel groups as proxies to pursue their international interests while avoiding direct involvement in an external armed conflict (Meier et al. 2022; Salehyan et al. 2011).

In contrast, the situation is fundamentally different for armed non-state principals. Armed non-state groups are likely to have comparatively smaller organizational capacity and military power than state actors (Aronson and Huth 2017). These capacity gaps, coupled with the fact that their domestic and international status is fundamentally politically and militarily contested, place them in a constant struggle for organizational survival and growth. By sponsoring other rebel groups, external armed non-state organizations can address their capacity gaps while attempting to increase their credibility and legitimacy both domestically and abroad (ibid.). For example, The National Patriotic Front of Liberia (NPFL) gained influence and importance in the broader West African region due to its support of the RUF in its fight against the government of Sierra Leone between 1993 and 1997 (Byman et al. 2001). As a result of this support, the NPFL was able to establish itself as a prominent actor in the region and gained significant international legitimacy. This legitimacy allowed the NPFL to participate in various peace talks and ceasefire negotiations, where it was able to advocate for its interests and exert its influence on the negotiations. Moreover, the NPFL's involvement in these negotiations helped to further increase its legitimacy and credibility, both domestically and abroad, as a key player in regional politics.

The struggle for survival and capacity gaps discussed above are common to both external rebel principals and rebel agents. Therefore, the relationship between principal and agents in the case of rebel groups is likely to be more balanced than that between a rebel group and a foreign state. Moghadam and Whyss (2020) go as far as claiming that "[f]or low–and moderate-capacity non-state sponsors, [...] the reliance on proxies is based more on need than on interest" (123). This more balanced relationship between the principal and the agent has important implications for the capacity and willingness of external non-state armed groups to affect the types of contentious political behaviours of their protégées. First, this more balanced relationship provides greater leverage to the supported armed organizations over external rebel supporters compared to foreign state supporters. As a result of this lower leverage, unlike state principals, external rebel supporters are likely to have lower expectations of the military success of their protégées. This is because defeating opponent regimes outright is difficult for any rebel group, whether principal or agent. Additionally, rebel principals are involved in their own local armed struggle against state coercive apparatuses and are unable to provide decisive military and organizational resources to their protégées. As opposed to outright military success, external rebel supporters might settle for their agents generating enough costs to be deemed credible threats. In other words, unlike foreign state supporters, external rebel supporters are more interested in their rebel protégées' demonstrations of credible commitment to wage war than in their military victories. Crucially, highly lethal terrorist campaigns can be used by rebel groups to signal their credible commitment to violent rebellion to external rebel supporters (Hovil and Werker 2005), increasing the legitimacy of the rebel principal while making future damage against the state more realistic (de Mesquita and Dickson 2007; Sanchez-Cuenca and De La Calle 2009).

Existing empirical literature identifies the lethality of terrorist attacks as one of the primary drivers of public attention and media coverage. For example, studies focusing on the United States find that substantial news space is occupied by domestic terrorist attacks with a higher number of fatalities (Chermak and Gruenewald 2006) and that every additional fatality leads to an average increase in media coverage of 46% (Kearns et al. 2019). There is also evidence that public attention to terrorism increases with more deadly terrorist attacks (Nussio et al. 2021). Ultimately, highly lethal terrorist violence signals resolve and commitment and raises the profile of a rebel group and its external rebel supporters. As discussed above, targeting non-combatants with terrorist violence is militarily cheaper than using direct attacks against state coercive apparatuses. Therefore, even rebel groups lacking sufficient military resources to engage successfully in conventional military violence can carry out highly lethal terrorist attacks capable of attracting substantial international attention and signal rebels' commitment to wage a costly rebellion. However, the causal arrow runs in both directions: external rebel supporters use screening mechanisms to identify rebel groups with preferences most similar to their own. Therefore, rebels that perpetrate, or are willing to perpetrate, more lethal terrorist violence and demonstrate credible commitment to a given cause might be more likely to attract external rebel group sponsors. On the other hand, rebels that receive support from external rebel groups are more likely to perpetrate more lethal terrorism to maintain their patrons' support while contributing towards increasing the political influence of their principals.

Below, I report an illustrative case study that provides initial qualitative support for the mechanism discussed in this subsection. The case of Al-Qaeda and Abu Sayyaf Group (ASG) provides evidence of two rebel groups engaged in a principal–agent relationship. The principal (Al-Qaeda) identifies the agent (ASG) as holding political preferences similar to its own. At the same time, the agent attracted the support of the principal by demonstrating commitment to the political cause: unable to inflict heavy costs on the government of the Philippines directly, ASG engaged in highly lethal terrorist campaigns. As soon as the patronage relationship between Al-Qaeda and ASG is disrupted, ASG changes its approach to terrorism: from highly lethal indiscriminate attacks against foreigners and the general population to targeted attacks against local politicians and kidnappings for ransom.

Case 4. Abu Sayyaf Group

The ASG emerged in the 1990s as a splinter group of the Moro National Liberation Front (MNLF), an armed movement led by multiple Muslim minority insurgent groups in the southern islands of the Philippines, which aimed to assert themselves against the Catholic majority. The breakaway group accused the MNLF to acquiesce too easily to a deal with the Philippine government when settling for an autonomous Muslim region in Mindanao and maintained that violent jihad was necessary to achieve a fully independent Islamic state (Counter Extremist Project 2007). The principal–agent relationship between Al-Qaeda and ASG emerged in the early years of ASG's foundation (Hammerberg and Faber 2017). The link between the two rebel groups was based on shared political objectives and personal trust between Osama Bin Laden and Ustadz Abdurajak Janjalani, the leader of the MNLF splintering groups and funder of the ASG. On the one hand, both organizations shared the conviction that violent jihad was necessary to achieve an independent Islamic state in their respective territories (Hammerberg and Faber 2017, 6). On the other hand, Abu Sayyaf, the founder of ASG, had developed a personal and direct relationship with Bin Laden and Bin Laden's brother-in-law in Pakistan, where he fought alongside them during the Soviet invasion of Afghanistan (Hammerberg and Faber 2017; Hutchison 2009).

Janjalani received military training in the late 1980s and into the 1990s at a training camp near Khost in Afghanistan. This camp was run by Abdur Rab Rasul Sayyaf, a religious scholar preaching a strict Wahhabi interpretation of Islam and supported by many affluent Saudis, including Bin Laden. At the camp, Janjalani developed the idea of waging jihad in his native Philippines with the aim of creating a pure Islamic state according to the precepts of Abdur Rab Rasul Sayyaf (Abuza 2002). In 1990, the ASG had already developed a regional reputation for engaging in terrorist attacks and kidnappings for ransom (Bale 2003). In 1991, Osama bin Laden became interested in providing military and financial support to the ASG, which was looking for external funders to sustain its armed campaign in the Philippines as a more stable financial base for its operations (Abuza 2002, 440). Bin Laden's motivation in financing the ASG was his goal of building a network of militant groups across the world to advance Al-Qaeda's Jihadist agenda. Bin Laden saw the ASG as a possible asset in its Jihadist campaign because the ASG had a close ideological stand and demonstrated the willingness to use violence to create an Islamic State (Gunaratna 2002). The same year, Bin Laden sent a top Al-Qaeda strategist, Ramzi Yousef, to the Philippines to train ASG's members in bomb-making in their camp on Basilan Island and support the ASG in its armed actions. Ramzi Yousef was introduced to the ASG's cadres as the 'emissary from Bin Laden' (Abuza 2002), suggesting that he also had monitoring functions within ASG on behalf of the leader of Al-Qaeda.

Soon after Ramzi Yousef's arrival, the ASG broadened its targets beyond Philippine coercive apparatuses to include the nation's Christian majority and citizens from the United States and other western countries (A. B. C. News 2001). The vast majority of ASG's violent attacks since the patron–agent relationship between Al-Qaeda and the ASG was established consisted of deadly indiscriminate bombings of civilian targets and kidnappings of foreign tourists. These attacks led to a total of 456 dead and injured civilians (Abuza 2002). There is evidence that under the direction of Ramzi Yousef, ASG plotted and committed increasingly lethal terrorist attacks, and that the driving motivation behind ASG's initial deadly terrorist campaign was Janjalani's ties to Al-Qaeda core, which provided ASG with financing and training (Fellman 2011). Beyon Ramzi Yousef, ASG received support from Al-Qaeda through Bin Laden's brother-in-law Muhammad Jamal Khalifa, who managed various charitable organizations that Al-Qaeda used as fronts for financing. Muhammad Jamal Khalifa was also dispatched to the Philippines in the 1990s, where he arranged trainings and funnelled money to ASG. In 1995, Ramzi Yousef, Muhammad Jamal Khalifa, and other Al-Qaeda members collaborated with the ASG in the Bojinka plot, in which 12 airplanes were to be bombed over the Pacific Ocean (Abuza 2005). However, a few months before the bombing, Ramzi Yousef was arrested in Pakistan and found responsible for the plot. During the investigation, it emerged that Muhammad Jamal Khalifa was also connected to the bombing plot and he was banned from returning to the Philippines (Fellman 2011).

As a consequence of these events, the Al-Qaeda–ASG relationship weakened substantially. The loss of financing and training from Al-Qaeda had a profound impact on the portfolio of violence of ASG and on the use of lethal terrorist attacks. Prior to the weakening of its connection with Al-Qaeda, ASG had carried out a number of high-profile attacks against Western targets in the Philippines, including bombings of civilian targets and kidnappings of foreign tourists (Abuza 2002). These attacks often resulted in significant casualties and generated extensive media attention. After losing support from Al-Qaeda, the ASG shifted its violent behaviours from highly lethal terrorist attacks to more discriminate kidnap-for-ransom attacks and other violent criminal activities against government officials and local businesses (Abuza 2002; Banoldi 2010). This suggests that the goal of the violence used by the ASG had shifted from enhancing the political status of its patron regionally and internationally through highly lethal and visible terrorist violence to ensuring their own organizational survival. Five years after the ban of Muhammad Jamal Khalifa, the Philippine National Security Advisor Rolio Golez declared to a local newspaper that there was "no evidence that Abu Sayyaf has gotten financing from Bin Laden recently. Otherwise, they would not have to resort to kidnappings" (Abuza 2002, 190).

4.2 Diasporas and NGOs

Diaspora groups are conceptualized here as communities of people with common national origins who have been displaced or voluntarily migrated from their country and have settled in other parts of the world (Cohen 2008). These communities regard themselves – and are regarded by others – as members of their country of origin, and this status is held regardless of their geographical location and citizenship (Shain 1994, 5). NGOs, on the other hand, are private organizations that operate independently of government control, typically established to promote a particular humanitarian cause or set of causes (Boli and Thomas 1999). Crucially, both diaspora groups and NGOs that directly support rebel organizations with money, diplomatic efforts, and/or recruitment typically share ethnic origins, familial links, ideological, and communal affinities with the populations in the territories where rebels operate (Byman et al. 2001; Collier et al. 1999). A well-known example of a rebel organization receiving substantial support from diaspora groups and NGOs all over the world is the Liberation Tigers of Tamil Eelam (LTTE). As of 1998, the LTTE received support from Tamil diasporas and NGOs based in 54 countries (Byman et al. 2001). For example, the LTTE's non-state supporters included the Australasian Federation of Tamil Associations, the Swiss Federation of Tamil Associations, the French Federation of Tamil Associations, the Federation of Associations of Canadian Tamils, the Ilankai Tamil Sangam in the United States, the Tamil Coordinating Committee in Norway, and the International Federation of Tamils in the United Kingdom (Chalk 1999).

Existing qualitative studies on the role of diaspora involvement in conflicts generally point to diaspora groups' role as peace-wreckers rather than peacemakers (Baser and Swain 2008, 47). These studies highlight the ways in which diaspora groups can obstruct conflict resolution and peacebuilding by making the conflicts more complex and difficult to resolve through negotiated settlements (Koinova 2013) and by polarizing political positions (Skrbiš 1999). However, other scholars have observed that cases in which diaspora groups actively incentivize political violence are fewer in comparison to cases in which diaspora actively engage in peace-making efforts (Baser and Swain 2008; Cochrane 2007; Newland 2018; Shain 1994). A more recent quantitative study also shows that diaspora support to rebels has positive implications for de-escalating civil wars' violence (Petrova 2019). Substantially less academic work exists on the effect that NGOs' direct support to rebels has on conflict dynamics. While some have claimed that NGOs generally do not have a high impact on insurgencies' behaviours (Byman et al. 2001, 96), anecdotal examples seem to suggest the contrary. For example, the military efficiency and success of the Afghan jihad during–and beyond – the Soviet-Afghan war, for example, can be traced back to the direct military and financial support of a worldwide network of sympathetic 'Islamic' NGOs (Kohlmann 2006).

Existing accounts suggest that the motivations of diaspora groups and NGOs in supporting rebel organizations significantly differ from those of foreign states and external rebel groups (Byman et al. 2001; Koinova 2013; Smith and Stares 2007). While foreign states support insurgencies to achieve their military objectives and external rebel groups support other rebels to strengthen their domestic and international political power, diaspora groups and NGOs support rebels to promote the interests of a particular community of people. Diaspora and NGOs typically mobilize to support rebel organizations in their homeland to protect their diaspora identity and homeland ties (Saideman and Ayres 2015). Their support is characteristically aimed at improving the situation of populations in civil war zones and shaping favourable long-term political outcomes for these populations (Byman et al. 2001; Koinova 2013; Smith and Stares 2007). In line with this idea, existing literature shows that in times of crisis such as civil wars, the activation of ties to homeland identity and the promotion of contributions to homeland stability and economic development are activated and fostered by the empathy and co-responsibility felt by members of diaspora groups towards their kin in the homeland (Cohen 2008; Desai and Kharas 2018; Safran 1991).

It is important to acknowledge that diaspora groups and NGOs are diverse groups with varying goals and different understandings of what favourable long-term political outcomes might mean. However, diaspora groups and NGOs that support rebel organizations are likely to be characterized by a strong aversion to highly lethal terrorist violence against the civilian population in conflict-affected areas, as minimizing physical insecurity and minimizing abuse from the government are necessary premises for promoting the interests of the community of people they identify with and aim to protect. In addition to directly endangering the physical security of local civilians, highly intense terrorist killings also motivate governmental retaliatory repression and the hardening of governments' negotiating positions, things that clearly diverge from the interests of diasporas and NGO principals. Diaspora groups may also have incentives to influence rebels' tactical choices of violence, leading them to reduce terrorism against civilians, as this would enable the return of diaspora members to their homeland without fear of becoming victims of civil war violence. This might be especially important for members of diasporas who reside abroad as a result of violent conflicts (Smith and Stares 2007). In line with the theoretical idea that support for rebels from non-state groups with familial, ethnic, ideological, and cultural links to populations in civil war zones discourages rebels' use of violence because it is contrary to their motives for supporting rebel organizations, Petrova (2019) found that diaspora groups, as supporters of insurgencies, increase the probability of rebels turning to nonviolent tactics instead of violent actions.

As in the case of support from external rebel organizations, the causal arrow is likely to run in both directions. On the one hand, diaspora and NGO supporters use screening mechanisms to identify rebel groups with preferences most similar to their own. Therefore, rebels that perpetrate or are willing to perpetrate less lethal terrorist violence against the local civilian population might be more likely to attract external diaspora groups and NGO sponsors. On the other hand, rebels that receive support from diaspora and NGOs are more likely to be sanctioned and lose the support they enjoyed when they use more lethal terrorist violence. Therefore, rebels that receive support from diaspora and NGOs are also more likely to preventively limit high levels of terrorist-related non-combatant deaths.

Next, I report an illustrative case study that provides initial qualitative support for the mechanism proposed in this subsection. The case of the Provisional Irish Republican Army (PIRA) provides evidence of a diaspora community and related NGOs with principal–agent relationships with a major rebel organization sharing with them ethnic and ideological ties. This illustrative case shows how the humanitarian NGO Irish Northern Aid (Noraid) and the Irish American diaspora put in place a system of screening and sanctioning mechanisms that allowed them to affect the IRA's use of lethal terrorist violence against civilians during the civil war in Northern Ireland.

Case 5. Provisional Irish Republican Army

The origins of the PIRA can be traced back to the Easter Rising of 1916, which was a rebellion against British rule staged by Irish rebels in Dublin. Although the uprising was ultimately unsuccessful, it mobilized support for the Irish independence movement and laid the basis for the formation of the Irish Republican Army (IRA) (English 2012). The IRA emerged as a paramilitary group committed to achieving a united, independent Ireland, and after the Irish War of Independence, which resulted in the establishment of the Irish Free State in 1922, the IRA split into various factions over the issue of whether to accept the partition of Ireland. The Provisional IRA, a faction that rejected the partition and continued to fight for a united Ireland, emerged then as a separate organization (Coogan 2000). The PIRA's armed campaign was most active in the 1970s and 1980s when it engaged in direct armed violence against British security forces and Protestant paramilitary groups in Northern Ireland. The wave of violence, which became known as the Troubles, resulted in thousands of deaths and caused widespread social and economic devastation (Thornton et al. 2004).

The PIRA's armed campaign against the British government in the 1970s and 1980s heavily depended on substantial acquisitions of weapons and financial resources obtained through the direct support of the Irish-American diaspora and various affiliated American-based NGOs, such as the Ancient Order of Hibernians (AOH) and subsequently the Irish Northern Aid Committee (Noraid). Irish-Americans, who had emigrated to the United States and their descendants, formed a substantial and influential community with strong ties to their ancestral homeland. The PIRA first made contact with the Irish-American diaspora in the early 1970s through a network of sympathizers and supporters in the United States (Dunnigan 2006). The PIRA's early contacts with the Irish-American diaspora were largely informal and took place through personal networks and grassroots campaigns (Cronin 2008). PIRA made use of existing Irish-American organizations, such as the AOH, to establish contacts and build support networks. The AOH had a long history of promoting Irish causes in the United States and was already well-established in Irish-American communities across the country. The PIRA's sympathizers within the AOH and other Irish-American organizations played a key role in connecting the PIRA with potential donors and supporters (Dunnigan 2006). As the PIRA's campaign intensified and its need for financing grew, more formal fundraising efforts were coordinated through the creation of new ad-hoc NGOs advocating for Irish reunification. Most notably, in the early 1970s, mobilized members of the Irish-American diaspora established Noraid. This NGO was particularly effective and raised millions of dollars that were channelled directly to PIRA while working as a lobby group for the cause of Irish reunification in the United States (Dunnigan 2006). The PIRA also worked to cultivate political support from Irish-American politicians and activists, who in turn helped to raise awareness of the conflict and put pressure on the U.S. government to take a more active role in seeking a resolution (Thornton et al. 2004).

Noraid routinely organized meetings between the Irish-American diaspora, PIRA Belfast Brigade Commander Joe Cahill, and other PIRA members who travelled to the United States to raise funds and procure arms (B. Anderson 2002; Moloney 2002,

2011; Wilson 1995). The meetings took place in pubs, churches, and social clubs, allowing the diaspora to scrutinize the behaviours and moral standing of the IRA and to assess the credibility of their image as freedom fighters (Brown 2015). To promote an image of the morality of their fight,

> IRA speakers (…) emphasized their links to the original Irish revolution and the progress of Irish self-determination. They eschewed direct references to bombs and the overtly socialist aspects of the Provisional IRA's platform. (…) Throughout the Troubles, Noraid thrived [in gathering weapons and financial resources] when the IRA appeared to have the moral high ground.
>
> (Brown 2015, 46)

The Irish-American diaspora and Noraid also sanctioned the PIRA when the organization appeared to endanger the physical security of the local population in Northern Ireland in connection to lethal terrorist attacks. For example, as a direct consequence of the Bloody Friday bombings in July 1972, fundraising declined, and high-level PIRA members were contacted by Noraid leaders with complaints about the killing of the civilian population (Wilson 1995). The influence of the Irish-American diaspora and its related NGOs on the use of lethal terrorist violence by the PIRA becomes evident when considering the statements of McClanahan, a high-level convicted PIRA bomber. McClanahan explains that the PIRA routinely warned local police forces to minimize civilian casualties in terrorist attacks to maintain support from the Irish diaspora and humanitarian NGOs in the United States:

> In the early years, I'm talking say 1970 until probably "76, '77, your main source of weapons was coming from the US … [W]hat I'm saying is bad politics plays bad in the bars and in the clubs of New York and wherever when you're asking for money to send back to the [P]IRA.
>
> (Brown 2015, 46)

5 Empirical Analysis

This chapter contains the empirical analysis that verifies the validity of the theoretical expectations of this study. Below, I summarize the main arguments and formulate a set of testable hypotheses departing from the theoretical exploration contained in Chapters 1, 3, and 4. The theoretical point of departure is that the leadership cadres of rebel organizations take rational decisions on the intensity of terrorism killings, weighing the benefits and the costs of targeting non-combatants with terrorist attacks against the financing needs of their organization. This is because the way in which rebel groups support their rebellion has significant consequences on the importance of legitimacy costs associated with using lethal terrorist violence against civilians. More specifically, the salience of the legitimacy costs of terrorist violence varies depending on the role that the local population plays in making internal and external financing available to rebel groups.

The reliance on any external actor for financing reduces the impact of legitimacy costs associated with killing local civilians in terrorist campaigns. Consequently, financing obtained from any external actor leads rebel groups to perpetrate more intense terrorist killings compared to financing obtained from or through local popular supporters. On the contrary, rebel groups that rely on external financing from natural resource exploitation face higher local legitimacy costs than rebels who obtain financing from any type of external actor. This is because natural resource exploitation is location specific. Therefore, rebels that rely on natural resource exploitation are more likely to refrain from intense civilian killings with terrorist violence. I derive that:

DOI: 10.4324/9781003377139-6

H1a: Rebel groups supported by foreign state actors are likely to perpetrate more intense terrorism killings than those who rely on local civilian support alone.

H1b: Rebel groups supported by external non-state actors are likely to perpetrate more intense terrorism killings than those who rely on local civilian support alone.

H1c: The magnitude of the effect of external non-state supporters is at least as big in size as the magnitude of the effect of foreign-state supporters.

H1d: The effect of natural resources on the likelihood of the lethality of terrorist attacks by rebel groups is not distinguishable from the effect of local civilian support.

The reliance on a more diverse range of external financing sources makes rebel groups less vulnerable to the consequences of alienating any one audience. As such, rebel groups with more diverse external financing sources can act more independently and use militarily cheaper violence such as terrorism to exert more pressure on their opponents and pursue their political goals without fearing consequences on their ability to survive as an organization and wage war. I derive that:

H2: Rebel groups relying on more diverse sources of external financing are likely to perpetrate more lethal terrorist attacks than rebels with fewer sources of external financing.

While overall the expectations on the effect of external actors' support on terrorism lethality might be valid, examining external non-state supporters in a disaggregated manner reveals that the salience of the costs of lethal terrorist violence differs across different types of external non-state actors. Financing from diaspora communities and NGOs is likely to decrease the use of lethal terrorist violence against non-combatants because they support rebel groups to minimize insecurity and shape favourable long-term political outcomes in conflict-affected areas. In contrast, external rebel group support is likely to increase the lethality of terrorist violence because rebel organizations support other armed groups to consolidate their international and domestic political influence and view highly lethal terrorist attacks as a measure of the credible commitment of their rebel protégées. Formally:

H3a: Rebel groups that receive support from external rebel groups are likely to perpetrate more intense terrorism killings than rebels with other types of financing.

H3b: Rebel groups that receive support from external NGOs and diasporas are likely to perpetrate less intense terrorism killings than rebels with other types of financing.

In the remaining of this chapter, I will explain the research design, present the operationalization of phenomena, and discuss the main results of the empirical analysis.

5.1 Research Design and Data

I test the hypotheses on a dataset composed by yearly observations on rebel organizations in civil wars. Periods of civil wars are identified when at least 25 battle-related deaths occur in a given country-year. The unit of analysis reflects the focus on rebel groups as rational actors making strategic decisions over the lethality of terrorism. The dataset comprises 204 rebel groups observed from 1989 to 2009 and contains information on rebel groups' number of terrorist-related deaths, battle-related deaths in conventional warfare, as well as external financing sources available to rebel groups in any given year of observation. To obtain this rich dataset, I extracted information from the Terrorist Organizations v.2014 2.0 (TORG) crosswalk (Asal et al. 2015); the Global Terrorist Database (GTD) by the National Consortium for the Study of Terrorism and Responses to Terrorism (START 2022); the Uppsala Conflict Data Program (UCDP) Dyadic Dataset v1-2015 (Harbom and Wallensteen 2007); the Non-State Actor Data 3.4 (NSA) (Cunningham and Gleditsch 2012; Cunningham et al. 2013); the UCDP Georeferenced Event Dataset 0.4 (GED) (Sundberg and Melander 2013); and the UCDP External Support Project–Primary Warring Party Dataset (Högbladh et al. 2011). I also use Rustad and Binningsbø (2012) to obtain data on rebel groups' natural resources exploitation in civil wars.

5.1.1 Dependent Variables

Terrorism killings intensity is measured through three alternative proxies. The main dependent variable – '*Terrorism killings intensity*' – is a ratio of terrorist-related non-combatant casualties to the total number of casualties: *Terrorism killings intensity = terrorism-related civilian causalities/(terrorism-related civilian casualties + battle-related deaths)*. To operationalized *Terrorism killings intensity*, I extract information on the number of victims of terrorist attacks from the GTD (START 2022) accounting for all GTD's inclusion criteria: 1) intentionality of the attacks; 2) use of violence or the threat of violence in the attacks; 3) attacks must be perpetrated by non-state actors; 4) attacks must be perpetrated for political, economic, or social goals; 5) perpetrators carry out attacks to coerce, threaten or transmit a message to a different audience than the victims; and 6) attacks target civilians or non-combatants and thus they violate international humanitarian laws. I extract yearly information on rebel groups' casualties in conventional armed violence from GED (Högbladh et al. 2011). I avoid the potential overlap between deaths coded in GTD and in UCDP GED, by retaining from GTD violent events deliberately targeting civilians with terrorist violence and excluding from GED conflict events between hostile rebel groups and one-sided violence.

I use a ratio of terrorist-related non-combatants casualties to the total number of casualties as the main proxy for the intensity of terrorism killings because this indicator allows us to distinguish in an explicit manner the strategic choice of deliberately targeting non-combatants with terrorist violence from the overall severity of civil wars violence. Crucially, using the total number of rebel groups' battle-related deaths to capture the rebel groups' strategic choice of targeting state coercive apparatuses implies that rebels can avoid such violence by terrain concealment or dispersion as often occurs in conflict where non-state armed actors are involved. *Terrorism killings intensity* ranges from 0 to 1. Zero indicates years in which the violence is conventional only, 1 indicates years in which rebel groups exclusively targeted non-combatants with terrorist violence while 0.5 indicated years in which the number of both types of killings is equal. Figure 5.1 shows the distribution of *Terrorism killings intensity*. It emerges that 58.68% of the observations correspond to years in which rebel groups exclusively cause the deaths of combatants, while 2.07% of the observations correspond to rebel groups-years with only terror-related non-combatant casualties. Years of exclusively terror-related non-combatant casualties are possible because rebels might participate

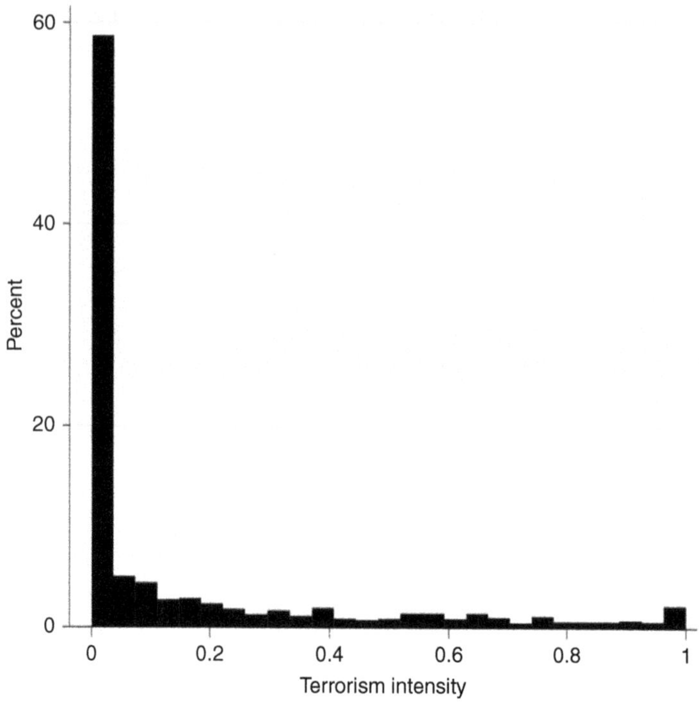

Figure 5.1 Terrorism killings intensity by rebel group-year.

in conventional battles without killing anyone. These observations correspond to years in which the 25 battle-related deaths necessary for inclusion in UCDP GED are caused by the state actor in the dyad or by other non-state armed actors in the same conflict. In a remarkable 25% of the observations, rebel groups killed more non-combatants with terrorism violence than combatants in conventional warfare.

I also use two alternative dependent variables as robustness checks. The first alternative dependent variable proxies the willingness of rebels to provoke a high number of non-combatant casualties with terrorist attacks and consists of a dichotomous indicator capturing the use of highly destructive explosives (for a similar approach see, Stanton 2013). *Highly destructive explosive* is equal to 1 if the rebels used grenades, mines, mail bombs, projectiles such as rockets mortars and missiles, remote explosive device, bombs carried bodily by human beings, time fuse, vehicle bombs, and other unknown explosive devices; equal to 0 otherwise. The use of highly destructive explosives represents a clear tactical choice of indiscriminate non-combatant targeting because rebel groups generally possess other, less sophisticated arms that allow a higher level of civilian targets' discrimination. Finally, I also use a dichotomous measure of '*Terrorism occurrence*' equal to 1 in years when rebel groups are reported to use terrorist tactics and 0 otherwise to test my theoretical prepositions against a measure that proxies the willingness of rebel groups to use terrorism.

5.1.2 Independent Variables

The main independent variables are dichotomous variables measuring rebel groups' sources of financing, including *Natural resources*, *Foreign state support*, and *External non-state support*. In addition, external non-state support is disaggregated into *External rebel groups' support* and *Diaspora and NGOs support*. Following the approach of Fortna et al. (2018), I assume, by elimination, that rebels with no access to support from foreign states and external non-state actors or natural resources are those who rely most heavily on the support of the local population. I use data from Rustad and Binningsbø (2012) to obtain information on whether rebels used natural resources to sustain their fight (see also Fortna et al. 2018). '*Natural resources*' is a dichotomous variable equal to one if natural resources provided income for the rebel groups including "precious gems, drugs, timber, crude oil, and other natural resources" (Fortna et al. 2018, 787). I do not use Lujala (2009) dataset on natural resources because it only provides information on whether natural resources are present in the conflict area and I do not use Walsh et al. (2018) dataset on natural resources because this dataset codes the modality of access to natural resources and therefore its variable 'extortion' captures a subset of cases of terrorist attacks (Walsh et al. 2018, 5).

To obtain the data on external support from foreign states and non-state actors and on support from external rebel groups, diaspora and NGOs, I manually coded information contained in the variables 'external_type_text' and 'external_code' from the

UCDP External Support Project Primary Warring Party Dataset (Högbladh et al. 2011): these variables "contains an English-language description of external supporters" (12). For example, for the Naxalite People War Group (PWG) who opposed India in 1992, I coded an instance of external rebel group support. In this case, the variable 'external_type_text' reports: "The PWG (...) had links with the Tamil separatist group Liberation Tigers of Tamil Eelam, and (...) the latter provided them with the equipment used by PWG for detonating explosives"; and the variable 'external_code' reports: 'LTTE: W [weapons] M [material/logistics]'. Another example is the Kurdistan Worker Party (PKK) that opposed Turkey in 1991. In this case, the variable 'external_codes' codes: '(...) Kurdish Diaspora: $ [money]'. I code instances of external financing that is alleged only if there is a clear indication of its kind and the supplier of the support is explicitly named. Beyond using textual information contained in the UCDP External Support Project Primary Warring Party Dataset (Högbladh et al. 2011), I integrate my data with information derived from academic case studies on specific rebel groups' financing sources. '*Foreign state support*' and '*External non-state support*' are two dichotomous variables equal to 1 when there is evidence that foreign state and external non-state actors, respectively, provided support to a rebel group in a given year. Non-state actors are defined as those actors that are not identifiable with the government of a country.

I generate a dichotomous variable measuring '*External financing*' equal to 1 when at least one type of external financing mentioned above is available to rebel groups in a given year. I also generate a count variable ranging from 0 to 3 measuring '*External financing diversity*' equal to the sum of the external financing sources available to rebel groups in a given year. Category 0 corresponds to cases where external financing is not observed, category 1 corresponds to cases where only one form of external financing is observed, and category 2 corresponds to cases where two out of the three possible types of external financing are observed. Observations with all three types of external financing contemporaneously present are coded as 3. Finally, I generate two dichotomous variables '*External rebel groups support*' and '*Diaspora and NGOs support*' equal to 1 when there is evidence that rebels receive support from diaspora groups and NGOs and external rebel groups, respectively, 0 otherwise.

5.1.3 Control variables

An obvious confounding variable is rebels' military strength. Support form external actors might be more likely provided to and accepted by moderately strong rebel groups (Salehyan et al. 2011). On the other hand, militarily weak rebels are more likely to use terrorist violence during civil wars (Polo and Gleditsch 2016; R. M. Wood 2010). '*Fighting capacity*' is a dichotomous item that extracts information from 'rebstrength' in the NSA (Cunningham et al. 2013). It takes the value of 1 when rebel groups are militarily 'weaker' or 'much weaker' than the opponent state, 0 otherwise.

I control for rebel groups territorial control. Even rebels that are weaker than the government they oppose may control terrain in remote regions where the state is feebler and exploit natural resources and local support in these peripheral areas. Territorial control may increase the cost of targeting civilians with terrorist attacks and rebels with territorial control might produce incentives to obtain resources locally rather than from transnational supporters. The proxy of '*Territorial control*' is a dichotomous measure, extracting information from the variable 'terrcont' in NSA (Cunningham and Gleditsch 2012; Cunningham et al. 2013). '*Territorial control*' is equal to 1 when rebel groups control territory and equal to 0 otherwise.

I control for state capacity. This is also likely to affect rebel groups' opportunity to obtain and exploit different sources of internal and external financing. Stronger states are likely to be better at controlling their natural resources and their borders and might be better able to block support from external actors. In turn, weak states that are unable to provide basic services may create grievances and affect the intensity of violent dissent and the use of terrorist violence (Crenshaw 1981; Piazza 2006). '*State capacity*' measures logged Real GDP per capita income of countries and it is extracted from Gleditsch (2002).

I also include a dichotomous measure of *Democracy* to control for regime type. This is a dichotomous variable equal to 1 when the positive converted *polity 2* score extracted from the Polity IV Project (Marshall et al. 2014) is equal or higher than 7, 0 for if it is smaller than 7. Transnational actors might be more constrained to provide support to insurgent movements in democratic states with legitimate institutions (Salehyan et al. 2011, 725). Democracies are also favourable environments for the use of terrorist strategies (Eubank and Weinberg 1994, 2001; Piazza 2006; Savun and Phillips 2009; Stanton 2013; Weinberg and Eubank 1998).

I control for the size of the population of the state extracting a logged measure of *Total population* from Gleditsch (2002). States with a larger population size experience a higher incidence of terrorist violence (Savun and Phillips 2009). Larger populations might also be correlated with higher opportunities for rebel groups to obtain local resources. Finally, I include a control for *Conflict intensity* in the models with binary outcome variables: terrorism occurrence and highly destructive explosive (see robustness checks in the Appendix). I introduce this measure to account for the level of civil war violence and I operationalize it as the total number of conventional casualties and extract this item from GED (Sundberg and Melander 2013).

5.2 Empirical Analysis

With the main dependent variables being a ratio ranging from 0 to 1, I estimate Papke and Wooldridge's (1996) model for fractional response variables. This is a generalized linear model with a logistic link.[1] I cluster standard errors by conflict dyad to account that the variance may differ systematically across pairs of warring parties. I also include a count of the number of years in which the lethality of terrorist attacks is twice the average together with the cubic polynomial of this indicator. Including these variables accounts for time dependence in the occurrence of extremely lethal use of terrorism. In fact, highly lethal terrorist attacks likely depend on rebels' organizational age and therefore are time-dependent (Carter and Signorino 2010; Clauset and Gleditsch 2012).

Figure 5.2 shows evidence for H1a, H1b, H1c, and H1d. While Model 1 focuses on the effect of the occurrence of external financing on the likelihood of *terrorism killings' intensity* compared to the effect of local civilian support, Models 2–4 show the individual disaggregated effects of different types of external financing, i.e. natural resources, foreign state support, and external non-state actors' support excluding from the sample observations that correspond to rebels with other types of external financing and, therefore, also having as baseline civilian support alone. In

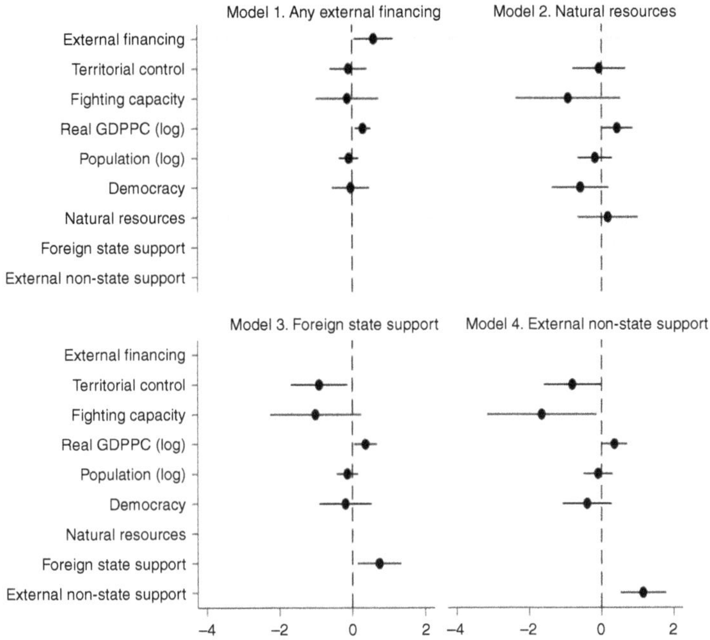

Figure 5.2 The effect of external financing on the terrorism killings intensity.
Note: The horizontal lines represent 95% confidence intervals.

line with the expectations of existing literature on external support and civilian victimization, Model 1 shows a positive and significant effect ($p<0.05$) of the presence of external financing on the likelihood of the lethality of terrorism. As expected, rebel groups relying on external financing are likely to perpetrate more lethal terrorist attacks than those who rely on local civilian support alone. Similarly, Models 3 and 4 show positive and significant effects of foreign states' support ($p<0.05$) and external non-state actors' support ($p<0.01$) on the likelihood of the lethality of terrorism. These results suggest that rebel groups relying exclusively on foreign state support or external non-state support are likely to perpetrate more intense terrorism killings than those who rely on local civilian support alone, according to my expectations. Model 2 shows no evidence that a similar positive relation is in

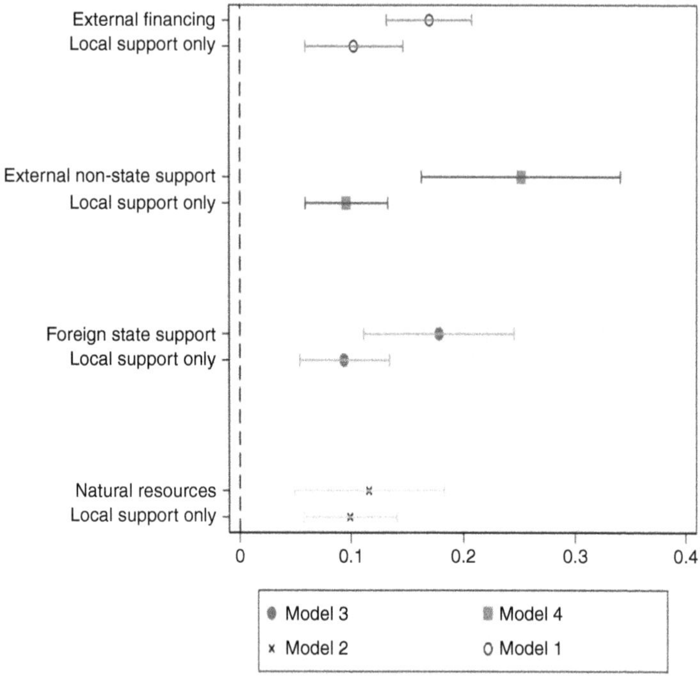

Figure 5.3 Marginal effects of the variables of interest on the expected terrorism killings intensity (from Figure 5.2).

Note: The horizontal lines represent 95% confidence intervals.

place for rebel groups relying exclusively on natural resources, suggesting that the effect of natural resources exploitation on the likelihood of the lethality of terrorism cannot be distinguished from the effect of local civilians' support.

Figure 5.3 plots the magnitudes of the effects of the variable of interests vs. the effect of local support for each of the four models presented in Figure 5.1. The results show that the magnitude of the effect of external non-state support is similar in size to the effect of foreign-state support providing evidence for H1c. Figure 5.2 also confirms that the effect of natural resources is statistically indistinguishable from the effect of local support.

Figure 5.4 presents two models that provide support for my expectations on the overall effects of the support of external

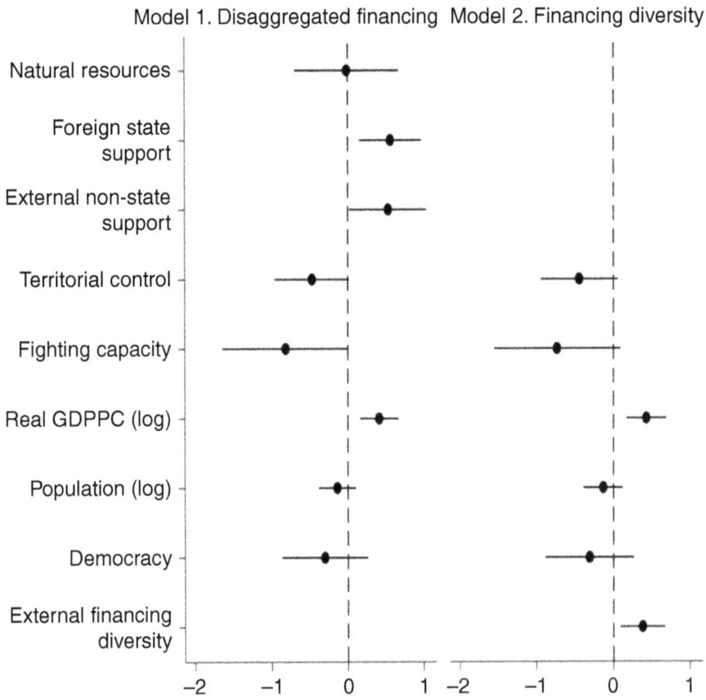

Figure 5.4 Effects of different types of external financing and external financing diversity on likelihood of terrorism killings intensity.

Note: The horizontal lines represent 95% confidence intervals.

actors and the diversity of sources of external financing (H2). Model 1 tests the individual effects of natural resources, support from foreign states, and external non-state actors considering the average effects of the other type of external financing simultaneously available to rebel groups in addition to the confounding variables already included in the analysis. The model shows that rebel groups with foreign state support and the support of external non-state actors are likely to perpetrate more intense terrorism killings ($p<0.01$ and $p<0.05$ respectively), while the average effect of natural resources on the likelihood of terrorism killings intensity is not distinguishable from 0. According to H2, Model 2 shows that rebels relying on more diverse sources of external financing

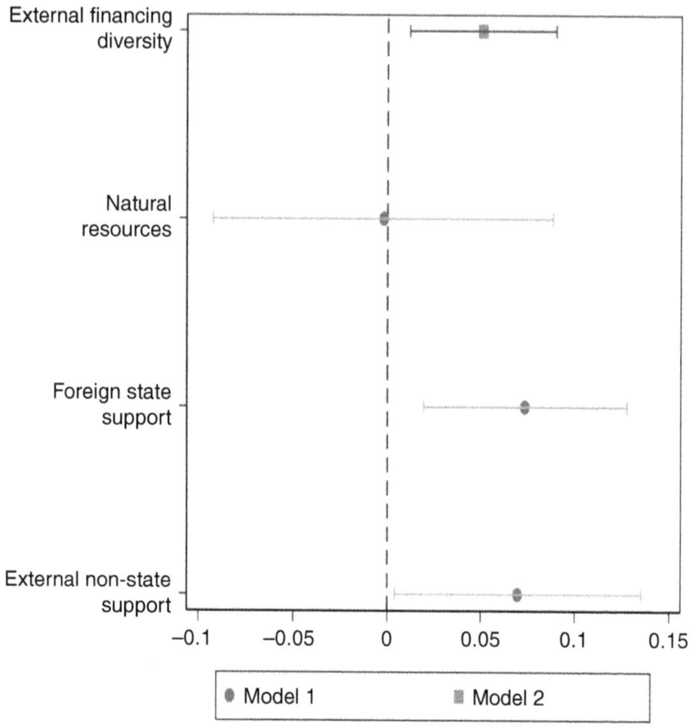

Figure 5.5 Marginal effects of the variables of interest on the expected terrorism killings intensity.

Note: The horizontal lines represent 95% confidence intervals.

are likely to perpetrate more lethal terrorism than those with fewer sources of external financing. The effect of external financing diversity is, as expected, positive and significant at $p<0.01$.

Figure 5.5 shows the magnitude of the effects of each variable of interests extracted from Models 1 and 2 in Figure 5.3. Differently from Figure 5.2, which plots the magnitude of the effect of the individual type of external financing with local support as a baseline, this figure shows the magnitude of the effects of every type of external financing accounting for the average effects of all other types of external financing simultaneously available to rebel groups. Collectively, and according to the comparative legitimacy costs theory presented above, Figures 5.4 and 5.5 show that the magnitude of the effect of support from external non-state actors is at least equal in size to the effect of support from foreign states. Figure 5.5 also suggests that the effect of external financing diversity is driven by the overall effects of the support of external actors rather than the reliance on natural resources since the overall effect of natural resources on the likelihood of the lethality of terrorism is indistinguishable from zero.

While at an aggregate level it appears that financing from external non-state actors increases the lethality of terrorism, disaggregating the effects of financing from diasporas and NGOs from financing from external rebel groups disclose a more nuanced picture: it provides evidence suggesting that the effect of different types of external non-state supporters vary depending on their different rationales when financing rebels. In Figure 5.6, Model 1 shows the disaggregated effects of the

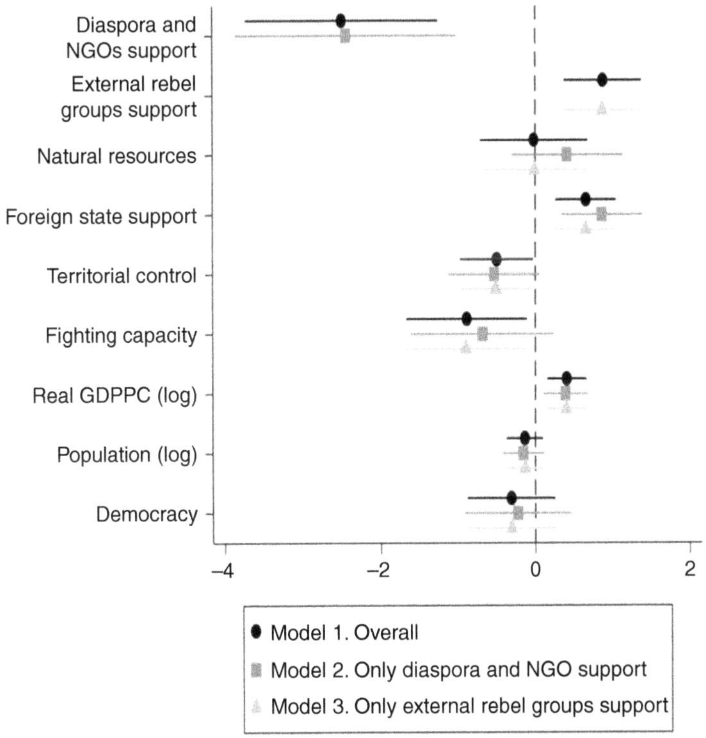

Figure 5.6 The effect of support from external rebel groups and diaspora and NGOs on terrorism killings intensity.

Note: The horizontal lines represent 95% confidence intervals.

support provided by diaspora and NGOs and external rebel groups taking into account simultaneously the average effects of the other type of external financing, i.e., foreign state support and natural resources in addition to the confounding variables already present in the analyses above. Model 2 tests the effect of support from diasporas and NGOs excluding from the sample observations that correspond to rebel groups that receive support also from external rebel groups. Vice versa, Model 3 tests the effect of support from external rebel groups excluding from the sample observations that correspond to rebel groups that receive support also from diasporas and NGOs. Figure 5.6 shows evidence in support of hypotheses H3a and H3b. Rebel groups with support from diasporas and NGOs are likely to perpetrate less intense terrorism killings and those with support from external rebel groups are likely to perpetrate more intense terrorism killings. Notably, the results reported for the effects of natural resources and state support in all three models are robust with the analyses presented in Figures 5.2–5.5.

Figure 5.7 shows that the marginal effects of support from diaspora and NGOs and support from external rebel groups remain largely unchanged across the model specifications reported in Figure 5.6. External rebel groups' support increases the intensity of terrorism killings by 11%. Although relatively large uncertainty can be observed, the magnitude of the negative effect of support from diaspora and NGOs on the intensity of terrorism killings is substantial: diaspora and NGOs support decreases the intensity of terrorism killings by 32% on average.

The only control variable with a robust and significant effect across the analysis is state capacity. Contrary to the expectation, however, higher state capacity, measured as real GDP per capita, is correlated with the likelihood of more intense terrorism killings. This might indicate that the relationship between state capacity and terrorist non-combatants targeting in civil wars is driven by rebels' considerations on the opportunities available to hurt the state indirectly rather than by grievances (Crenshaw 1981; Piazza 2006). The findings above remain robust across a wide range of robustness checks (36 additional models). In particular, the main findings do not change when excluding all control variables (Appendix, Figures A.1– A.6) and they are also robust to using OLS as an alternative functional form

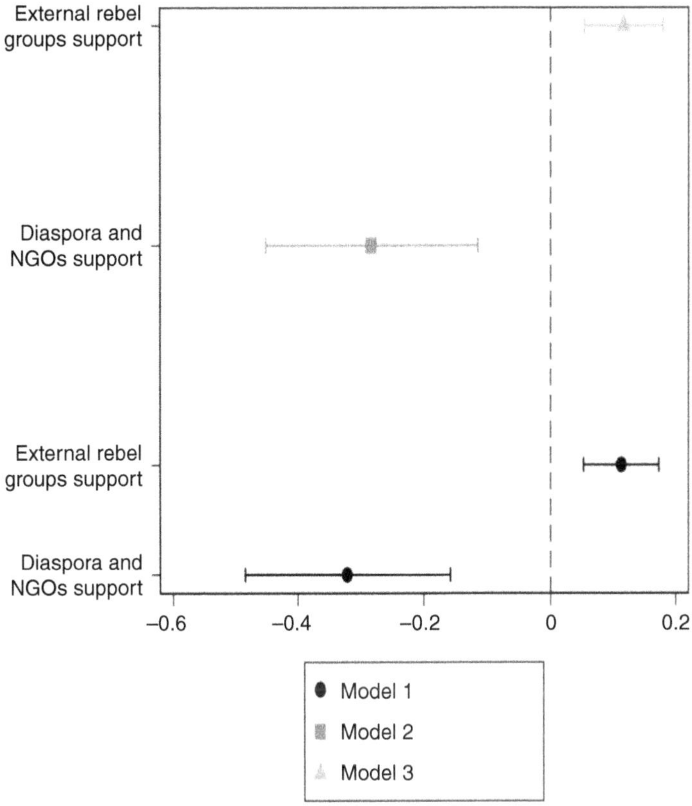

Figure 5.7 Marginal effects of the variables of interest on terrorism killings intensity (from Figure 5.6).

Note: The horizontal lines represent 95% confidence intervals.

(Appendix, Figures A.7–A.9). All the main findings remain virtually unchanged when using logit models to test the hypotheses on terrorism occurrence (Appendix, Figures A.10–A.15) and highly destructive explosive (Appendix, Figures A.16–A.21) as alternative dependent variables. It is worth mentioning that the effect of natural resources became positive and significant across all models regressed on terrorism occurrence and that this is in accordance with the findings presented in Fortna et al. (2018).

This result suggests that rebel groups financing their rebellion through natural resources might be willing to use terrorism as a repertoire of violence but might limit the lethality of terrorist attacks.

Note

1 I do not use a beta link because it is incapable of accounting for the zeros that represent 60% of the observations in the outcome variable.

Conclusions for Theory and Policy

Summary of the Empirical Results

Based on my empirical analyses, it appears that the various sources of financing employed by insurgent organizations to fuel their armed campaigns carry considerable weight in terms of determining the salience of the legitimacy costs associated with employing lethal terrorist tactics against civilian populations. My first set of results pertains to the comparative effects of different external financing sources, accounting for the role that the local population plays in making internal and external financing available to rebel groups. The most important corroborated claims are that while external non-state actors' support to rebel groups increases the lethality of terrorism (H1b), the effect of external financing obtained through the exploitation of natural resources on the lethality of terrorism is not distinguishable from the effect of internal financing obtained through the support of the local population (H1d). I also found that the magnitude of the effects of financing on terrorism lethality is similar across external actors: support from foreign states, as well as external non-state actors, increases the lethality of terrorism by rebel groups in civil wars similarly (H1a, H1c). In line with these findings, my analysis also shows that the positive effect of the existence of external financing on the intensity of terrorism killings in civil wars is primarily driven by the support of external actors rather than by the exploitation of natural resources as a means to financing rebellion. More diverse financing sources available to rebel groups also increase the lethality of terrorism they use in civil wars (H2). This set of relationships aligns with the expectations given my

DOI: 10.4324/9781003377139-7

theoretical comparative framework and its postulated implications for different individual external financing sources. However, when zooming in on the investigation of the role of the support provided by external non-state actors, the empirical findings suggest that the effect of different types of non-state actor supporters depends on their specific interests when financing a rebel organization. As expected, in line with the existing knowledge on rebel groups and diasporas and NGOs' motivations for supporting far-away rebel organizations, the empirical analysis shows that the support of diaspora groups and NGOs decreases the lethality of terrorism used by rebel groups in civil wars (H3a) and that the support of external rebel groups increases the lethality of terrorism used by rebel groups in civil wars (H3b).

Theoretical Significance

By focusing on how rebel organizations' various sources of external financing affect the lethality of terrorism in civil wars, this study adds to the literature on terrorism in civil wars, which has primarily investigated the roles of rebels' characteristics, civil war's internal dynamics, and the structural characteristics of the opponent state. By focusing on all external financing sources available to rebels, this study expands the scope of the literature on terrorism in civil wars beyond domestic correlates to the international arena. This study also contributes to advancing existing knowledge on the relationship between external financing to rebel groups and civilian victimization. This literature has so far focused on foreign states' support and natural resources exploitation. By focusing on the role played by the support of different types of external non-state actors, this study expands the scope of the literature on financing and civilian victimization beyond the scope of more traditional Security Studies. This is significant because, since the end of the Cold War, external non-state actors such as diasporas, NGOs, and rebel movements are gaining a prominent role in fostering and sustaining rebel groups in their fights (Byman et al. 2001; Collier et al. 1999).

While the theoretical mechanism connecting the effect of external financing to the salience of the legitimacy costs of targeting non-combatants with terrorism used here reflects the consensual mechanism in existing works on rebels' financing and violence, comparing the implications of individual external financing sources available, often simultaneously, to rebels for the cost–benefit calculus that rebels make when taking strategic decisions on the lethality of terrorist violence, leads to novel testable conclusions. When considering the role played by the local population in making individual types of external financing available and comparing across external financing sources, it becomes clear that financing from any external actors decreases the salience of the impact of the costs of terrorism for local legitimacy, with implications for rebel groups' survival, when compared to financing from the local population or natural resources. The implication is that rebel groups with external non-state actors' support are likely to perpetrate more intense terrorism killings than those with local civilian support alone, and that the effect of the support of external non-state actors is at least as salient as the effect of the support of foreign states when it comes to terrorism killing intensity. Departing from the same theoretical premises, a higher diversity of external financing sources leads to a higher lethality of terrorism, as losing anyone external source of financing yields fewer implications on the ability of rebel groups to wage war and survive as an organization. However, the positive effect of more diverse external financing sources on the intensity of terrorism lethality appears to be primarily driven by the support of external actors, rather than by the exploitation of natural resources. In fact, when disaggregating the effects of different forms of external financing and accounting for the simultaneous availability of different sources of external financing explicitly in the empirical analyses, the effect of natural resources is, at best, not robust across model specifications.

This study also highlights the importance of considering the motives of external actors' support and offers novel insights by disaggregating the effect of support provided by different types of external non-state actors. I demonstrate that the effect of external non-state funders on the lethality of terrorism is informed by principal–agent dynamics and varies depending on the goals of specific external non-state actors when supporting rebel organizations. In particular, diasporas and NGOs are characterized by a strong aversion to the use of terrorist violence against non-combatants, as minimizing physical insecurity and abuse from the government are necessary premises for achieving their objectives of improving the status of populations in civil war zones and shaping favourable long-term political outcomes for these populations. External rebel groups, on the other hand, perceive the higher lethality of terrorist violence as a signal that their rebel protégées are willing and capable of generating enough costs to be deemed credible threats to local security. Therefore, the use of highly intense terrorism killings by rebel protégées is seen by external rebel supporters as an efficient way to promote their international status. According to my expectations, I find that support from diasporas and NGOs correlates with the likelihood of less intense terrorism killings, while support from external rebel groups correlates with the likelihood of more intense terrorism killings.

Policy Relevance

> Conflict researchers often motivate the importance of their work by claiming that their research has important policy implications', but the proposals offered are often at best incomplete. (…) [Typically], a number of common limitations (…) [underly] claims about policy implications, including a lack of discussion of objectives and priorities, stating objectives themselves as if they were policies, claims about targeting factors without discussing the effectiveness of possible interventions, and a failure to consider uncertainty and potential tensions with other objectives or unintended effects.
>
> (Gleditsch 2023, 1)

In this sub-section, I will try to avoid these problems, and, rather than providing incomplete policy recommendations, I will discuss current objectives and priorities of counter-insurgency operations and depict a picture of the ways in which this study might be helpful to inform policy debates on the actions to prioritize in counter-insurgencies assuming that they aim at protecting local civilians in civil wars.

Any existing counter-insurgency doctrines emphasize the importance of disrupting external financing to sustain insurgencies. For example, the US Army's Field Manual on Counterinsurgency (Nagl et al. 2015) assumes that disrupting an insurgency's financial support system is critical to the success of counter-insurgency operations. The manual suggests that counter-insurgency forces should focus on cutting off the flow of external financing to rebel groups and preventing them from accessing other sources of financing, such as criminal activities or local support. Similarly, the NATO Allied Joint Doctrine for Counterinsurgency (COIN) (NATO 2002) recognizes the importance of disrupting external financing and claims that to defeat an insurgency, it is necessary to cut off its financial and material support from internal or external sources. This doctrine recommends that counter-insurgency forces should target the financial networks of insurgent groups and disrupt their ability to access external sources of financing. Major counterinsurgency doctrines also recognize the connection between financial support for insurgent groups and their ability and willingness to perpetrate violence against civilians. For example, the US Army's Field Manual on Counterinsurgency (Nagl et al. 2015) notes that targeting insurgent financing sources can impact the security of local populations. The manual recognizes that cutting off external financing for insurgent groups can reduce their ability to carry out attacks against civilians and decrease their influence in local communities. Crucially, the COIN (NATO 2002) also recognizes that disrupting external financing for insurgent groups can provide a direct and measurable impact on civilian security. However, existing doctrines fail to recognize the potential impact of targeted efforts to isolate insurgents from specific sources of external financing on securing the local population.

This study suggests that the debate on the efforts to isolate rebels from their sources of external financing should focus on establishing priorities for intervention according to the risks that different external financing sources imply for the security of the local population. These risks should be understood as an implication of the involvement that the local population has in making any given external financing source available to rebels, the diversity of external financing sources available, and the motivations of external supporters when providing financing to rebels. The empirical findings of this study suggest that, since support from foreign states and external rebel groups correlates with more intense terrorism killings, isolating rebels from these financing sources should be given priority over isolating them from diasporas and NGOs or from the access to natural resources. In line with the findings of Petrova (2019), my empirical analysis also suggests that counter-insurgency operations might actually benefit from diplomatic efforts that make diasporas and NGOs part of political solutions of civil conflicts. Interestingly, the fact that diasporas and NGOs' support to rebel organizations is consistently associated with lower lethality of terrorist violence suggests perhaps that more external unarmed non-state actors should be engaged in conflict management.

While counter-insurgency doctrines might recognize the potential importance of targeted efforts to isolate insurgents from specific sources of external financing, there may be challenges in implementing effective policies that aim at protecting civilians through the isolation of the rebels to specific external financing sources. For example, it can be difficult to identify and target specific external sources of financing, especially if rebel groups are able to operate in areas beyond the reach of counter-insurgency forces and receive the financing from external rebel groups in safe havens geographically distant from the conflict areas. Additionally, disrupting the external financing system of insurgent groups may have unintended consequences, such as pushing rebel groups towards more illicit/criminal activities or alienating local populations who may rely on them for economic support. Therefore, counter-insurgency operations are faced with fundamental conundrums and must carefully consider the potential impact of their actions on both the external financing system of rebel groups and the local populations they seek to protect.

Bibliography

ABC News. 2001. 'The Abu Sayyaf-Al Qaeda Connection'. *ABC News*. https://abcnews.go.com/International/story?id=79205&page=1 (April 19, 2023).

Abdullah, Ibrahim. 1998. 'Bush Path to Destruction: The Origin and Character of the Revolutionary United Front/Sierra Leone'. *Journal of Modern African Studies* 36(2): 203–35.

———. 2007. 'The Making of the Sierra Leonean Tragedy'. In Ashgate, 63–85.

Abuza, Zachary. 2002. 'Tentacles of Terror: Al Qaeda's Southeast Asian Network'. *Contemporary Southeast Asia* 24(3): 427–65.

———. 2005. *Balik Terrorism: The Return of the Abu Sayyaf*. Fort Belvoir, VA: Defense Technical Information Center. www.dtic.mil/docs/citations/ADA439349 (April 21, 2023).

Aljazeera. 2023, 21 July. *What Role Do Outside Players Have in the War in Sudan?* www.aljazeera.com/program/inside-story/2023/4/21/what-role-do-outside-players-have-in-the-war-in-sudan

Anderson, Brendan. 2002. *Joe Cahill: A Life in the IRA*. Reprint edition. Dublin: O'Brien Press.

Anderson, Noel. 2019. 'Competitive Intervention, Protracted Conflict, and the Global Prevalence of Civil War'. *International Studies Quarterly* 63(3): 692–706.

Arjona, Ana. 2016. *Rebelocracy*. Cambridge University Press.

Aronson, Jacob, and Paul K. Huth. 2017. 'The Size of Rebel and State Armed Forces in Internal Conflicts: Measurement and Implications'. In *Peace and Conflict 2017*, Routledge.

Asal, Victor, Ken Cousins, and Kristian Skrede Gleditsch. 2015. 'Making Ends Meet: Combining Organizational Data in Contentious Politics'. *Journal of Peace Research* 52(1): 134–38.

Asal, Victor, and R. Karl Rethemeyer. 2008. 'The Nature of the Beast: Organizational Structures and the Lethality of Terrorist Attacks'. *Journal of Politics* 70(2): 437–49.

Aydin, Aysegul, and Patrick M. Regan. 2012. 'Networks of Third-Party Interveners and Civil War Duration'. *European Journal of International Relations* 18(3): 573–97.

Bale, Jeffry. 2003. *The Abu Sayyaf Group in Its Philippine and International Contexts*. Middlebury Institute of International Studies. www.middlebury.edu/institute/sites/www.middlebury.edu.institute/files/2023-03/baleASGreport.pdf?fv=uIWgXfJR.

Banoldi, Rommel C. 2010. 'The Sources of the Abu Sayyaf's Resilience in the Southern Philippines'. *CTC Sentinel* 3(5): 17–19.

Basedau, Matthias, and Jann Lay. 2009. 'Resource Curse or Rentier Peace? The Ambiguous Effects of Oil Wealth and Oil Dependence on Violent Conflict'. *Journal of Peace Research* 46(6): 757–76.

Baser, Bahar, and Ashok Swain. 2008. 'Diasporas as Peacemakers: Third Party Mediation in Homeland Conflicts'. *International Journal on World Peace* 25(3): 7–28.

Beckett, Ian F. 2001. *Modern Insurgencies and Counter-Insurgencies: Guerrillas and Their Opponents since 1750*. 1st edition. London; New York: Routledge.

Belgioioso, Margherita. 2018. 'Going Underground: Resort to Terrorism in Mass Mobilization Dissident Campaigns'. *Journal of Peace Research* 55(5): 641–55.

Belgioioso, Margherita, and Ches Thurber. 2023. 'From Doctrine to Detonation: Ideology, Competition, and Terrorism in Campaigns of Mass Resistance'. *Journal of Peace Research*: 00223433221135338.

Berman, Nicolas, Mathieu Couttenier, Dominic Rohner, and Mathias Thoenig. 2017. 'This Mine Is Mine! How Minerals Fuel Conflicts in Africa'. *American Economic Review* 107(6): 1564–1610.

Biddle, Stephen, and Jeffrey A. Friedman. 2008. *The 2006 Lebanon Campaign and the Future of Warfare: Implications for Army and Defense Policy*. Strategic Studies Institute, US Army War College. www.jstor.org/stable/resrep12091.6 (April 19, 2023).

Billon, Philippe Le. 2013. *Fuelling War: Natural Resources and Armed Conflicts*. London: Routledge.

Boli, John, and George M. Thomas, eds. 1999. *Constructing World Culture: International Nongovernmental Organizations Since 1875*. 1st edition. Stanford, CA: Stanford University Press.

Brenner, David. 2018. 'Inside the Karen Insurgency: Explaining Conflict and Conciliation in Myanmar's Changing Borderlands'. *Asian Security* 14(2): 83–99.

Brown, Joseph Matthew. 2015. '*The Bomber Who Calls Ahead: Terrorism, Insurgency, and the Politics of Pre-Attack Warnings*'. Columbia University. https://doi.org/10.7916/D8JD4W3R (April 19, 2023).

Bueno de Mesquita, Ethan. 2013. 'Rebel Tactics'. *Journal of Political Economy* 121(2): 323–57.

Buhaug, Halvard, Scott Gates, and Päivi Lujala. 2009. 'Geography, Rebel Capability, and the Duration of Civil Conflict'. *Journal of Conflict Resolution* 53(4): 544–69.

Byman, Daniel et al. 2001. *Trends in Outside Support for Insurgent Movements.* RAND Corporation. www.rand.org/pubs/monograph_reports/MR1405.html (April 19, 2023).

Carter, David B., and Curtis S. Signorino. 2010. 'Back to the Future: Modeling Time Dependence in Binary Data'. *Political Analysis* 18(3): 271–92.

Chalk, Peter. 1999. *Liberation Tigers of Tamil Eelam's (LTTE) International Organization And Operations – A Preliminary Analysis.* https://irp.fas.org/world/para/docs/com77e.htm

Chenoweth, Erica, and Kurt Schock. 2015. 'Do Contemporaneous Armed Challenges Affect the Outcomes of Mass Nonviolent Campaigns?'. *Mobilization: An International Quarterly* 20(4): 427–51.

Chermak, Steven M., and Jeffrey Gruenewald. 2006. 'The Media's Coverage of Domestic Terrorism'. *Justice Quarterly* 23(4): 428–61.

Clauset, Aaron, and Kristian Skrede Gleditsch. 2012. 'The Developmental Dynamics of Terrorist Organizations'. *PLOS ONE* 7(11): e48633.

Cochrane, Feargal. 2007. 'Irish-America, the End of the IRA's Armed Struggle and the Utility of "Soft Power"'. *Journal of Peace Research* 44(2): 215–31.

Cochrane, Feargal, Bahar Baser, and Ashok Swain. 2009. 'Home Thoughts from Abroad: Diasporas and Peace-Building in Northern Ireland and Sri Lanka'. *Studies in Conflict & Terrorism* 32(8): 681–704.

Cohen, Robin. 2008. *Global Diasporas: An Introduction.* 2nd edition. London: Routledge.

Colaresi, Michael. 2014. 'With Friends Like These, Who Needs Democracy? The Effect of Transnational Support from Rivals on Post-Conflict Democratization'. *Journal of Peace Research* 51(1): 65–79.

Collier, Paul, Anke Hoeffler, and Paul Collier. 1999. *Greed and Grievance in Civil War.* The World Bank. https://elibrary.worldbank.org/doi/abs/10.1596/1813-9450-2355 (April 20, 2023).

Coogan, Tim Pat. 2000. *The I. R. A.* Revised edition. London: HarperCollins.

Counter Extremist Project. 2007. *Abu Sayyaf Group (ASG).* www.counterextremism.com/threat/abu-sayyaf-group-asg

Crenshaw, Martha. 1981. 'The Causes of Terrorism'. *Comparative Politics* 13(4): 379–99.

Cronin, M. 2008. 'The Influence of the Irish American Diaspora on American Foreign Policy toward Ireland'. *Journal of Policy History* 20(3): 339–62.

Cunningham, David E. 2010. 'Blocking Resolution: How External States Can Prolong Civil Wars'. *Journal of Peace Research* 47(2): 115–27.

———. 2016. 'Preventing Civil War: How the Potential for International Intervention Can Deter Conflict Onset'. *World Politics* 68(2): 307–40.

Cunningham, David E., and Kristian Skrede Gleditsch. 2012. 'Codebook for the Non-State Actor Data'. www.essex.ac.uk/~ksg/data/NSAEX_codebook.pdf.

Cunningham, David E., Kristian Skrede Gleditsch, and Idean Salehyan. 2013. 'Non-State Actors in Civil Wars: A New Dataset'. *Conflict Management and Peace Science* 30(5): 516–31.

Dasgupta, Anindita. 2012. 'Resisting the Resistance: Civilian Protests against ULFA Insurgency in Assam, India'. *Millennial Asia* 3(2): 115–37.

Davis, Jessica. 2013. 'Evolution of the Global Jihad: Female Suicide Bombers in Iraq'. *Studies in Conflict & Terrorism* 36(4): 279–91.

Denly, Michael et al. 2022. 'Do Natural Resources Really Cause Civil Conflict? Evidence from the New Global Resources Dataset'. *Journal of Conflict Resolution* 66(3): 387–412.

Desai, Raj M., and Homi Kharas. 2018. 'What Motivates Private Foreign Aid? Evidence from Internet-Based Microlending'. *International Studies Quarterly* 62(3): 505–19.

Dudek, Nicholas. 2021. 'Understanding Violence by Non-State Armed Groups: The Case of the RUF'. *Civil Wars* 23(3): 371–95.

Dudouet, Véronique, and Janel B. Galvanek. 2018. 'Financing Armed Groups during Ceasefires'. *Norwegian Centre for Conflict Resolution.* https://noref.no/Publications/Themes/Peacebuilding-and-mediation/Financing-armed-groups-during-ceasefires (April 20, 2023).

Duffield, Mark. 2002. 'War as a Network Enterprise: The New Security Terrain and Its Implications'. *Cultural Values* 6(1–2): 153–65.

Dunnigan, J. 2006. 'The Irish-American Diaspora and the Provisional IRA'. *Journal of Irish and Scottish Studies* 1(1): 19–35.

Eck, Kristine, and Lisa Hultman. 2007. 'One-Sided Violence Against Civilians in War: Insights from New Fatality Data'. *Journal of Peace Research* 44(2): 233–46.

Enders, Walter, and Todd Sandler. 2011. *The Political Economy of Terrorism.* 2nd edition. Cambridge: Cambridge University Press. www.cambridge.org/core/books/political-economy-of-terrorism/08A7A2B70F52CE80489CBBCA9D96E949 (April 19, 2023).

English, Richard. 2012. *Armed Struggle: The History of the IRA*. Reprint edition. Pan.

Erbrick, Stephen. 2012. *Economization of the Sierra Leone War*. https://core.ac.uk/download/pdf/228636065.pdf.

Eubank, William Lee, and Leonard Weinberg. 1994. 'Does Democracy Encourage Terrorism?' *Terrorism and Political Violence* 6(4): 417–35.

———. 2001. 'Terrorism and Democracy: Perpetrators and Victims'. *Terrorism and Political Violence* 13(1): 155–64.

Fair, C. Christine. 2005. 'Diaspora Involvement in Insurgencies: Insights from the Khalistan and Tamil Eelam Movements'. *Nationalism and Ethnic Politics* 11(1): 125–56.

Fellman, Zac. 2011. *Case Study*. Center for Strategic & International Studies. https://csis-website-prod.s3.amazonaws.com/s3fs-public/legacy_files/files/publication/111128_Fellman_ASG_AQAMCaseStudy5.pdf.

Findley, Michael G., and Joseph K. Young. 2012. 'Terrorism and Civil War: A Spatial and Temporal Approach to a Conceptual Problem'. *Perspectives on Politics* 10(2): 285–305.

Fortna, Virginia Page. 2015. 'Do Terrorists Win? Rebels' Use of Terrorism and Civil War Outcomes'. *International Organization* 69(3): 519–56.

Fortna, Virginia Page, Nicholas J. Lotito, and Michael A. Rubin. 2018. 'Don't Bite the Hand That Feeds: Rebel Funding Sources and the Use of Terrorism in Civil Wars'. *International Studies Quarterly* 62(4): 782–94.

Gberie, Lansana. 2005. *A Dirty War in West Africa: The R.U.F. and the Destruction of Sierra Leone*. London: C Hurst.

Gleditsch, Kristian Skrede. 2002. 'Expanded Trade and GDP Data'. *Journal of Conflict Resolution* 46(5): 712–24.

———. 2023. '"This Research Has Important Policy Implications…"'. *Peace Economics, Peace Science and Public Policy* 29(1): 1–17.

Gohain, Hiren. 2007. 'Chronicles of Violence and Terror: Rise of United Liberation Front of Asom'. *Economic and Political Weekly* 42(12): 1012–18.

Goodhand, Jonathan. 2008. 'Corrupting or Consolidating the Peace? The Drugs Economy and Post-Conflict Peacebuilding in Afghanistan'. *International Peacekeeping* 15(3): 405–23.

Gunaratna, Rohan. 2001. *Terrorism and Small Arms*. New York.

———. 2002. *Inside Al Qaeda: Global Network of Terror*. Scribe Publications.

Hammerberg, P. Kathleen, and Pamela G. Faber. 2017. *Abu Sayyaf Group (ASG): An Al-Qaeda Associate Case Study*. www.cna.org/archive/CNA_Files/pdf/dim-2017-u-016122-2rev.pdf.

Hancock, Landon E., and Christopher Roger Mitchell. 2007. *Zones of Peace*. Kumarian Press.

Harbom, Lotta, Erik Melander, and Peter Wallensteen. 2008. 'Dyadic Dimensions of Armed Conflict, 1946–2007'. *Journal of Peace Research* 45(5): 697–710.

Harbom, Lotta, and Peter Wallensteen. 2007. 'Armed Conflict, 1989—2006'. *Journal of Peace Research* 44(5): 623–34.

Hazen, Jennifer M. 2013. *What Rebels Want: Resources and Supply Networks in Wartime*. Ithaca, NY; London: Cornell University Press.

Hinkkainen Elliott, Kaisa, and Joakim Kreutz. 2019. 'Natural Resource Wars in the Shadow of the Future: Explaining Spatial Dynamics of Violence during Civil War'. *Journal of Peace Research* 56(4): 499–513.
Högbladh, Stina, Therése Pettersson, and Lotta Themnér. 2011. 'UCDP External Support Project Primary Warring Party Dataset Codebook v. 1.0-2011'.
Hovil, Lucy, and Eric Werker. 2005. 'Portrait of a Failed Rebellion: An Account of Rational, Sub-Optimal Violence in Western Uganda'. *Rationality and Society* 17: 5–34.
Hultquist, Philip. 2013. 'Power Parity and Peace? The Role of Relative Power in Civil War Settlement'. *Journal of Peace Research* 50(5): 623–34.
Human Rights Watch. 2000. *Sierra Leone*. www.hrw.org/legacy/wr2k1/africa/sierraleone.html.
———. 2005. *Youth, Poverty and Blood*. www.hrw.org/report/2005/04/13/youth-poverty-and-blood/lethal-legacy-west-africas-regional-warriors (April 21, 2023).
Humphreys, Macartan, and Jeremy M. Weinstein. 2006. 'Handling and Manhandling Civilians in Civil War'. *American Political Science Review* 100(3): 429–47.
Hutchison, Billye G. 2009. *Abu Sayyaf*. US Air Force Counterproliferation Center. https://media.defense.gov/2019/Apr/11/2002115513/-1/-1/0/49ABUSAYYAF.PDF
Jentzsch, Corinna. 2014. 'Militias and the Dynamics of Civil War–ProQuest'. www.proquest.com/openview/86f2f654634ab83b14a29e64da92cea1/1?cbl=18750&pq-origsite=gscholar&parentSessionId=thAh5LuA380AQwQeBMgl5dsB%2FycS4r5FAVEU6H5BHHY%3D (April 20, 2023).
Johansson, Karin, and Mehwish Sarwari. 2019. 'Sexual Violence and Biased Military Interventions in Civil Conflict'. *Conflict Management and Peace Science* 36(5): 469–93.
Jolliffe, Kim. 2016. 'Ceasefires, Governance and Development: The Karen National Union in Times of Change'.
Jones, Benjamin T. 2017. 'Altering Capabilities or Imposing Costs? Intervention Strategy and Civil War Outcomes'. *International Studies Quarterly* 61(1): 52–63.
Kaldor, Mary. 2012. *New and Old Wars: Organized Violence in a Global Era*. Polity Press. www.polity.co.uk/book.asp?ref=9780745655635 (April 19, 2023).
Kalyvas, Stathis N. 2006. *The Logic of Violence in Civil War*. Cambridge: Cambridge University Press. www.cambridge.org/core/books/logic-of-violence-in-civil-war/3DFE74EA492295FC6940D58CA8EF4D5C (April 19, 2023).
Kaplan, Oliver. 2013. 'Protecting Civilians in Civil War: The Institution of the ATCC in Colombia'. *Journal of Peace Research* 50(3): 351–67.

Karen News. 2012. 'KNU to Close down Antimony Mining Companies'. *Karen News*. https://karennews.org/2012/04/knu-to-close-down-antimony-mining-companies/ (April 19, 2023).

Karlén, Niklas. 2017. 'The Legacy of Foreign Patrons: External State Support and Conflict Recurrence'. *Journal of Peace Research* 54(4): 499–512.

Kearns, Erin M., Allison E. Betus, and Anthony F. Lemieux. 2019. 'Why Do Some Terrorist Attacks Receive More Media Attention Than Others?' *Justice Quarterly* 36(6): 985–1022.

Keels, Eric, Jay Benson, and Michael Widmeier. 2021. 'Teaching from Experience: Foreign Training and Rebel Success in Civil War'. *Conflict Management and Peace Science* 38(6): 696–717.

Keen, David. 1998. 'The Economic Functions of Violence in Civil Wars (Special Issue)'. *Adelphi Papers* 38(320): 1–89.

Kohlmann, Evan F. 2006. *The Role of Islamic Charities in International Terrorist Recruitment and Financing*. Danish Institute for International Studies. www.jstor.org/stable/resrep13293 (April 19, 2023).

Koinova, Maria. 2013. 'Four Types of Diaspora Mobilization: Albanian Diaspora Activism For Kosovo Independence in the US and the UK'. *Foreign Policy Analysis* 9(4): 433–53.

Koubi, Vally, Gabriele Spilker, Tobias Böhmelt, and Thomas Bernauer. 2014. 'Do Natural Resources Matter for Interstate and Intrastate Armed Conflict?' *Journal of Peace Research* 51(2): 227–43.

Kruk, Edit. 2020. 'Sierra Leone's Revolutionary United Front and Its Violence: Liberia's Charles Taylor, Colonial Legacies, and Oppressive Rule'. *Strife*. www.strifeblog.org/2020/07/20/sierra-leones-revolutionary-united-front-and-its-violence-liberias-charles-taylor-colonial-legacies-and-oppressive-rule/ (April 21, 2023).

Kumar, Praveen. 2004. 'External Linkages and Internal Security: Assessing Bhutan's Operation All Clear'. *Strategic Analysis* 28(3): 390–410.

Kydd, Andrew H., and Barbara F. Walter. 2006. 'The Strategies of Terrorism'. *International Security* 31(1): 49–80.

Lederach, John Paul. 2005. 'The Challenge of Terror: A Traveling Essay.' *Peace and Conflict Studies* 12(2): Article 6. DOI: 10.46743/1082-7307/2005.1065. https://nsuworks.nova.edu/pcs/vol12/iss2/6

Levi, Margaret. 1989. *Of Rule and Revenue*. University of California Press, 1988. www.jstor.org/stable/10.1525/j.ctt1pngtk

Lidow, Nicholai Hart, ed. 2016. 'Frontmatter'. In *Violent Order: Understanding Rebel Governance through Liberia's Civil War*. Cambridge: Cambridge University Press, i–iv. www.cambridge.org/core/books/violent-order/frontmatter/7407B90FA3798C7C5BE7CFAF34FFE27E (April 19, 2023).

Lujala, Paivi. 2009. 'Deadly Combat over Natural Resources: Gems, Petroleum, Drugs, and the Severity of Armed Civil Conflict'. *Journal of Conflict Resolution* 53(1): 50–71.

Lyall, Jason, and Isaiah Wilson. 2009. 'Rage Against the Machines: Explaining Outcomes in Counterinsurgency Wars'. *International Organization* 63(1): 67–106.

Malan, Mark et al. 2005. *Sierra Leone: Building the Road to Recovery*. Lynne Rienner. www.africaportal.org/publications/sierra-leone-building-the-road-to-recovery/.

Marshall, Monty G., Ted R. Gurr, and K. Jaggers. 2014. 'Polity IV Project: Political Regime Characteristics and Transitions, 1800–2013. Version: P4v2014'. www.systemicpeace.org/inscr/p4manualv2016.pdf.

Meier, Vanessa, Niklas Karlén, Therése Pettersson, and Mihai Croicu. 2022. 'External Support in Armed Conflicts: Introducing the UCDP External Support Dataset (ESD), 1975–2017'. *Journal of Peace Research*: 00223433221079864.

de Mesquita, Ethan Bueno, and Eric S. Dickson. 2007. 'The Propaganda of the Deed: Terrorism, Counterterrorism, and Mobilization'. *American Journal of Political Science* 51(2): 364–81.

Mitton, Kieran. 2015. *Rebels in a Rotten State: Understanding Atrocity in the Sierra Leone Civil War*. 1st edition. Oxford University Press.

Moghadam, Assaf, and Michel Wyss. 2020. 'The Political Power of Proxies: Why Nonstate Actors Use Local Surrogates'. *International Security* 44(4): 119–57.

Moloney, Ed. 2002. *A Secret History of the Ira*. 1st edition. New York: W. W. Norton.

———. 2011. *Voices from the Grave: Two Men's War in Ireland*. Main edition. London: Faber & Faber.

Monlar, Andrew R., Tinker Jerry R., and LeNoir Jhon D. 1966. *Human Factors Considerations of Undergrounds in Insurgencies*. https://apps.dtic.mil/sti/citations/AD0645518 (April 20, 2023).

Muro, Diego, ed. 2020. *When Does Terrorism Work?* 1st edition. Routledge.

Nagl, John A., David H. Petraeus, and Sarah Sewall. 2015. *The U.S. Army/Marine Corps Counterinsurgency Field Manual*. Reprint edition. Echo Point Books & Media.

Nathan, Laurie, Karl DeRouen Jr., and Marie O. Lounsbery. 2018. 'Civil War Conflict Resolution from the Perspectives of the Practitioner and the Academic'. *Peace Change* 43: 344–70. https://doi.org/10.1111/pech.12301

NATO. 2002. 'Allied Joint Doctrine for Counter-Insurgency (COIN)'. https://assets.publishing.service.gov.uk/government/uploads/system/uploads/attachment_data/file/1082608/20220504-AJP_3_27_A_COIN.pdf.

Newland, Kathleen. 2018. 'Voice After Exit: Diaspora Advocacy'.

Newman, Edward. 2007. 'Weak States, State Failure, and Terrorism'. *Terrorism and Political Violence* 19(4): 463–88.

Nussio, Enzo, Tobias Böhmelt, and Vincenzo Bove. 2021. 'Do Terrorists Get the Attention They Want?' *Public Opinion Quarterly* 85(3): 900–12.

Olson, Mancur. 1993. 'Dictatorship, Democracy, and Development'. *American Political Science Review* 87(3): 567–76.

Papke, Leslie E., and Jeffrey M. Wooldridge. 1996. 'Econometric Methods for Fractional Response Variables with an Application to 401(k) Plan Participation Rates'. *Journal of Applied Econometrics* 11(6): 619–32.

Peters, Krijn. 2011. *War and the Crisis of Youth in Sierra Leone*, ed. Stephanie Kitchen. Cambridge: Cambridge University Press. https://www.cambridge.org/core/books/war-and-the-crisis-of-youth-in-sierra-leone/B022BC412BD991E3B86B572113F98FD5 (April 19, 2023).

Petrova, Marina G. 2019. 'What Matters Is Who Supports You: Diaspora and Foreign States as External Supporters and Militants' Adoption of Nonviolence'. *Journal of Conflict Resolution* 63(9): 2155–79.

Piazza, James A. 2006. 'Rooted in Poverty? Terrorism, Poor Economic Development, and Social Cleavages'. *Terrorism and Political Violence* 18(1): 159–77.

Polo, Sara M. T., and Belén González. 2020. 'The Power to Resist: Mobilization and the Logic of Terrorist Attacks in Civil War'. *Comparative Political Studies* 53(13): 2029–60.

Polo, Sara M. T., and Kristian Skrede Gleditsch. 2016. 'Twisting Arms and Sending Messages: Terrorist Tactics in Civil War'. *Journal of Peace Research* 53(6): 815–29.

Record, Jeffrey. 2009. *Beating Goliath: Why Insurgencies Win*. Washington, DC: Potomac Books.

Regan, Patrick M., and M. Scott Meachum. 2014. 'Data on Interventions during Periods of Political Instability'. *Journal of Peace Research* 51(1): 127–35.

Richards, Paul. 1998. *Fighting for the Rain Forest: War, Youth & Resources in Sierra Leone*. Reprinted edition. www.cabdirect.org/cabdirect/abstract/19980606307 (April 21, 2023).

———. 2002. 'Wars and Violent Conflicts in West Africa'. In *West Africa: An Introduction to Its History, Civilization and Contemporary Situation*. Cambridge; New York; London: Cambridge University Press.

Roberts, Jordan. 2019. 'Targeting and Resistance: Reassessing the Effect of External Support on the Duration and Outcome of Armed Conflict'. *Civil Wars* 21(3): 362–84.

Ross, Michael L. 2004. 'What Do We Know about Natural Resources and Civil War?' *Journal of Peace Research* 41(3): 337–56.

Roth, Amanda. 2015. '[The Role of Diasporas in Conflict | Semantic Scholar'. *Journal of International Affairs* 68: 289.

Rubin, Michael A. 2020. 'Rebel Territorial Control and Civilian Collective Action in Civil War: Evidence from the Communist Insurgency in the Philippines'. *Journal of Conflict Resolution* 64(2–3): 459–89.

Rustad, Siri Aas, and Helga Malmin Binningsbø. 2012. 'A Price Worth Fighting for? Natural Resources and Conflict Recurrence'. *Journal of Peace Research* 49(4): 531–46.

Safran, William. 1991. 'Diasporas in Modern Societies: Myths of Homeland and Return'. *Diaspora: A Journal of Transnational Studies* 1(1): 83–99.

Saideman, Stephen, and R. William Ayres. 2015. *For Kin or Country: Xenophobia, Nationalism, and War*. Reprint edition. New York: Columbia University Press.

Saikia, Jaideep. 2012. 'Autumn in Springtime The ULFA Battles for Survival'. www.satp.org/satporgtp/publication/faultlines/volume7/Fault7-JaideepSF.htm#_ftnref10 (April 19, 2023).

Salehyan, Idean, David Siroky, and Reed M. Wood. 2014. 'External Rebel Sponsorship and Civilian Abuse: A Principal-Agent Analysis of Wartime Atrocities'. *International Organization* 68(3): 633–61.

Salehyan, Idean, Kristian Skrede Gleditsch, and David E. Cunningham. 2011. 'Explaining External Support for Insurgent Groups'. *International Organization* 65(4): 709–44.

Sanchez-Cuenca, Ignacio, and Luis De La Calle. 2009. 'Domestic Terrorism: The Hidden Side of Political Violence'. 12: 31–49.

Sanjoy, Hazarika. 1995. *Strangers of the Mist: Tales of War And Peace from India's Northeast*. 1st edition. New Delhi: Penguin.

Savun, Burcu, and Brian J. Phillips. 2009. 'Democracy, Foreign Policy, and Terrorism'. *Journal of Conflict Resolution* 53(6): 878–904.

Sawyer, Katherine, Kathleen Gallagher Cunningham, and William Reed. 2017. 'The Role of External Support in Civil War Termination'. *Journal of Conflict Resolution* 61(6): 1174–1202.

Schelling, Thomas C. 2009. Arms and Influence: With a New Preface and Afterword. New Haven, CT: Yale University Press.

Schubiger, Livia Isabella. 2021. 'State Violence and Wartime Civilian Agency: Evidence from Peru'. *Journal of Politics* 83(4): 1383–98.

Schultz, Kenneth A. 2010. 'The Enforcement Problem in Coercive Bargaining: Interstate Conflict over Rebel Support in Civil Wars'. *International Organization* 64(2): 281–312.

Schultze-Kraft, Markus. 2017. 'Understanding Organised Violence and Crime in Political Settlements: Oil Wars, Petro-Criminality and

Amnesty in the Niger Delta'. *Journal of International Development* 29(5): 613–27.

Shain, Yossi. 1994. 'Ethnic Diasporas and U.S. Foreign Policy'. *Political Science Quarterly* 109(5): 811–41.

Sjoberg, Laura. 2013. *Gendering Global Conflict: Toward a Feminist Theory of War*. Columbia University Press.

Sjoberg, Laura, and Jessica Peet. 2011. 'A (Nother) Dark Side of the Protection Racket'. *International Feminist Journal of Politics* 13(2): 163–82.

Skaperdas, Stergios. ' Economics and Conflict: The Dark Side of Self-Interest And Its Governance as Economic Activities'.

Skrbiš, Zlatko. 1999. *Long-Distance Nationalism: Diasporas, Homelands and Identities*. 1st edition. Brookfield, VT: Routledge.

Smith, Hazel, and Paul Stares. 2007. *Diasporas in Conflict: Peace-Makers or Peace-Wreckers?* UNU Press. https://collections.unu.edu/view/UNU:2481 (April 21, 2023).

Snyder, Richard. 2006. 'Does Lootable Wealth Breed Disorder?: A Political Economy of Extraction Framework'. *Comparative Political Studies* 39(8): 943–68.

Stanton, Jessica A. 2013. 'Terrorism in the Context of Civil War'. *Journal of Politics* 75(4): 1009–22.

START. 2022. 'Global Terrorism Database 1970–2020 [Data File]'. www.start.umd.edu/gtd.

Steenkamp, Christina. 2017. 'The Crime-Conflict Nexus and the Civil War in Syria'. 6(1): 11.

Sundberg, Ralph, and Erik Melander. 2013. 'Introducing the UCDP Georeferenced Event Dataset'. *Journal of Peace Research* 50(4): 523–32.

Testerman, Matthew. 2015. 'Removing the Crutch: External Support and the Dynamics of Armed Conflict'. *Studies in Conflict & Terrorism* 38(7): 529 42.

Thomas, Jakana. 2014. 'Rewarding Bad Behavior: How Governments Respond to Terrorism in Civil War'. *American Journal of Political Science* 58(4): 804–18.

Thornton, Chris, Seamus Kelters, Brian Feeney, and David McKittrick. 2004. *Lost Lives: The Stories of the Men, Women and Children Who Died as a Result of the Northern Ireland Troubles*. 2nd edition. Edinburgh: Mainstream Publishing.

Tilly, Charles, Sidney Tarrow, Charles Tilly, and Sidney Tarrow. 2015. *Contentious Politics*. Second Edition. Oxford; New York: Oxford University Press.

Toft, Monica Duffy, and Yuri M. Zhukov. 2015. 'Islamists and Nationalists: Rebel Motivation and Counterinsurgency in Russia's North Caucasus'. *American Political Science Review* 109(2): 222–38.

Truth and Reconciliation Commission of Sierra Leone (TRC). 2004. *Final Report*. www.sierraleonetrc.org/index.php/view-the-final-report/table-of-contents.

UN Security Council. 2000. *Final Report of the Panel of Experts on Sierra Leone Established Pursuant to Security Council Resolution 1306*. United Nations.

Valentino, Benjamin, Paul Huth, and Dylan Balch-Lindsay. 2004. '"Draining the Sea": Mass Killing and Guerrilla Warfare'. *International Organization* 58(2): 375–407.

Viterna, Jocelyn. 2014. *Dynamics of Political Violence: A Process-Oriented Perspective on Radicalization and the Escalation of Political Conflict*. Surrey: Ashgate.

Vorrath, Judith. 'From War to Illicit Economies: Organized Crime and State-Building in Liberia and Sierra Leone'.

Walsh, James Igoe, Justin M. Conrad, Beth Elise Whitaker, and Katelin M. Hudak. 2018. 'Funding Rebellion: The Rebel Contraband Dataset'. *Journal of Peace Research* 55(5): 699–707.

Walsh, James Igoe, and James A. Piazza. 2010. 'Why Respecting Physical Integrity Rights Reduces Terrorism'. *Comparative Political Studies* 43(5): 551–77.

Weinberg, Leonard B., and William L. Eubank. 1998. 'Terrorism and Democracy: What Recent Events Disclose'. *Terrorism and Political Violence* 10(1): 108–18.

Weinstein, Jeremy M. 2007. *Inside Rebellion: The Politics of Insurgent Violence*. Illustrated edition. Cambridge; New York: Cambridge University Press.

Whitaker, Beth Elise, James Igoe Walsh, and Justin Conrad. 2019. 'Natural Resource Exploitation and Sexual Violence by Rebel Groups'. *Journal of Politics* 81(2): 702–6.

Wickham-Crowley, Timothy. 2015. 'Dal Gobierno de Abajo al Gobierno de Arriba … and Back: Transitions to and from Rebel Governance in Latin America'. In *Rebel Governance*. Cambridge University Press, 47–73.

Wilson, Andrew J. 1995. *Irish America and the Ulster Conflict, 1968–1995*. Washington, D.C.: Catholic University of America Press.

Wood, Elisabeth Jean. 2003. *Insurgent Collective Action and Civil War in El Salvador*. Cambridge: Cambridge University Press. www.cambridge.org/core/books/insurgent-collective-action-and-civil-war-in-el-salvador/70D35F82CEEB47F2F14957EE31B5BFD6 (April 19, 2023).

Wood, Reed M. 2010. 'Rebel Capability and Strategic Violence against Civilians'. *Journal of Peace Research* 47(5): 601–14.

———. 2014. 'Opportunities to Kill or Incentives for Restraint? Rebel Capabilities, the Origins of Support, and Civilian Victimization in Civil War'. *Conflict Management and Peace Science* 31(5): 461–80.
Woods, Kevin M. 2018. *The Conflict Resource Economy and Pathways to Peace in Burma*. United States Institute of Peace.

Appendix

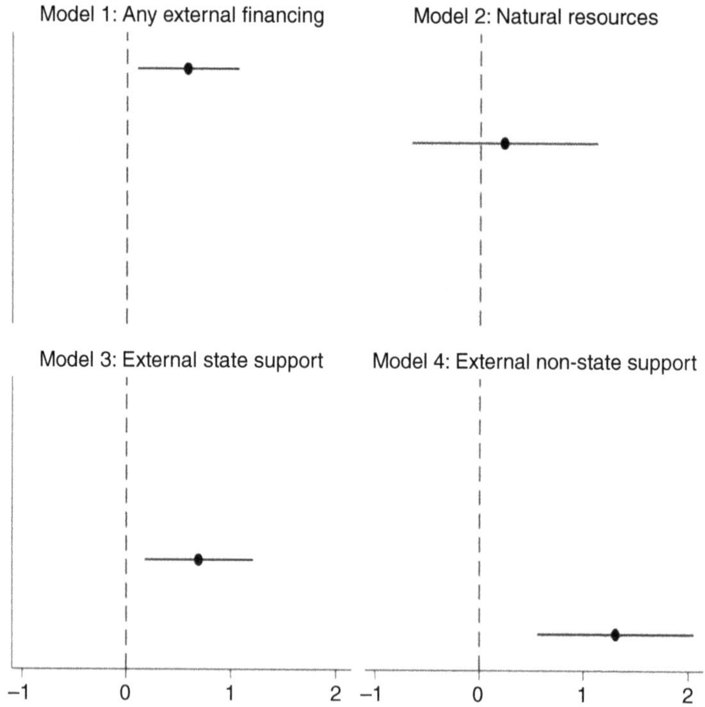

Figure A.1 The effect of external financing on the likelihood of lethality of terrorism (binomial models).

Note: The horizontal lines represent 95% confidence intervals.

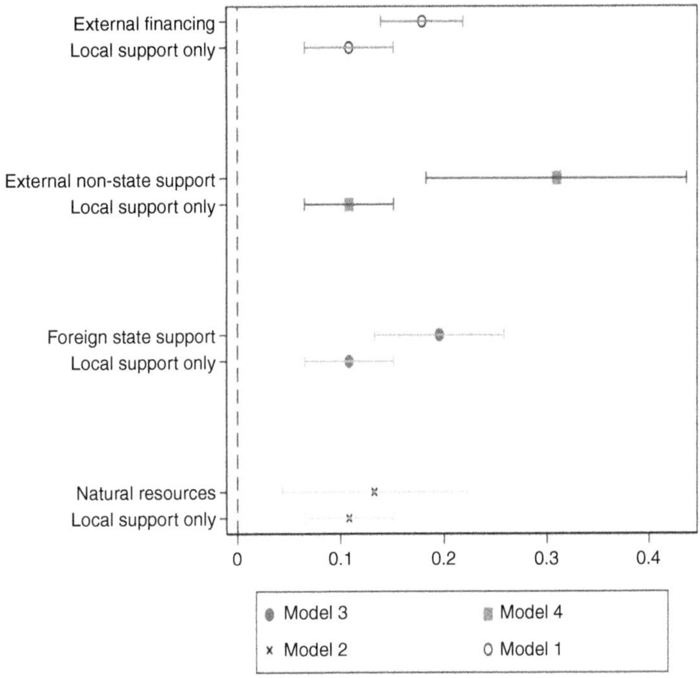

Figure A.2 Marginal effects of the variables of interest on the expected lethality of terrorism (binomial models from Figure 5.1).

Note: The horizontal lines represent 95% confidence intervals.

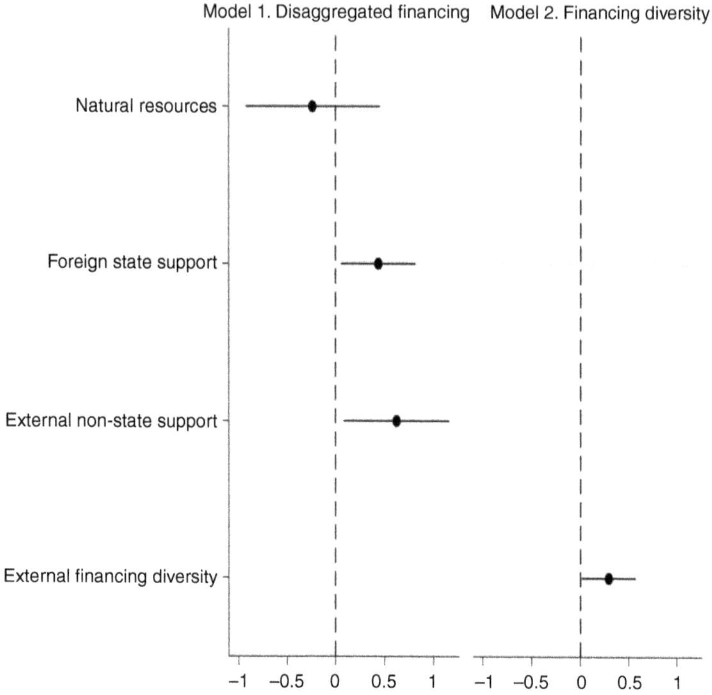

Figure A.3 Effects of different types of external financing and external financing diversity on likelihood of lethality of terrorism (binomial models).

Note: The horizontal lines represent 95% confidence intervals.

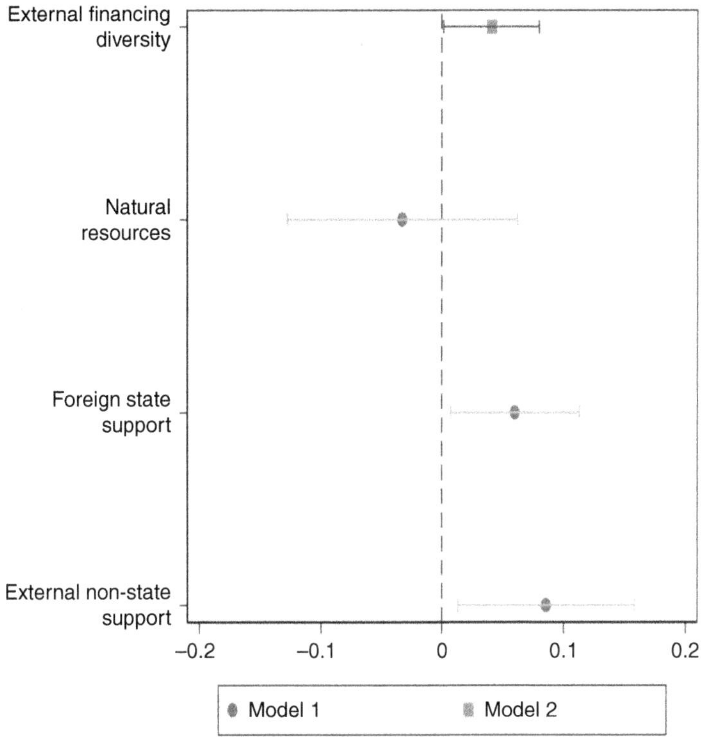

Figure A.4 Marginal effects of the variables of interest on the expected lethality of terrorism (binomial models from Figure 5.3).

Note: The horizontal lines represent 95% confidence intervals

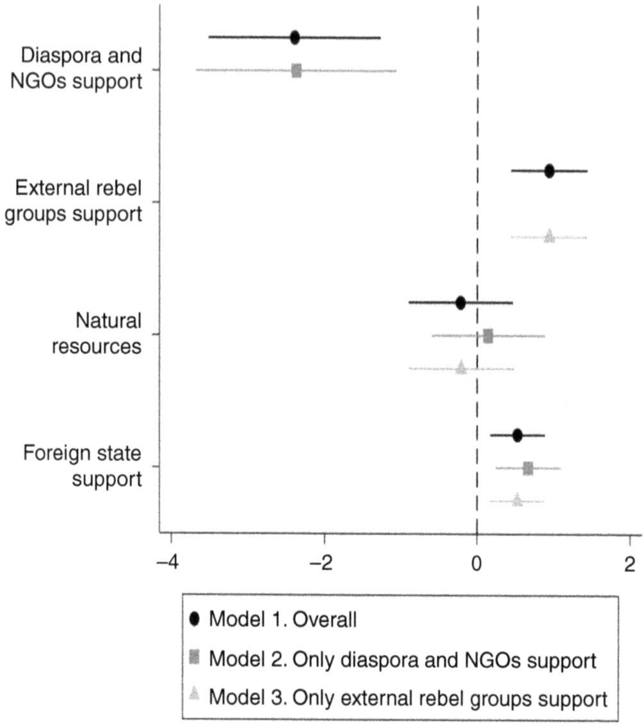

Figure A.5 The effect of types of external non-state supporters on terrorism intensity (binomial models).

Note: The horizontal lines represent 95% confidence intervals

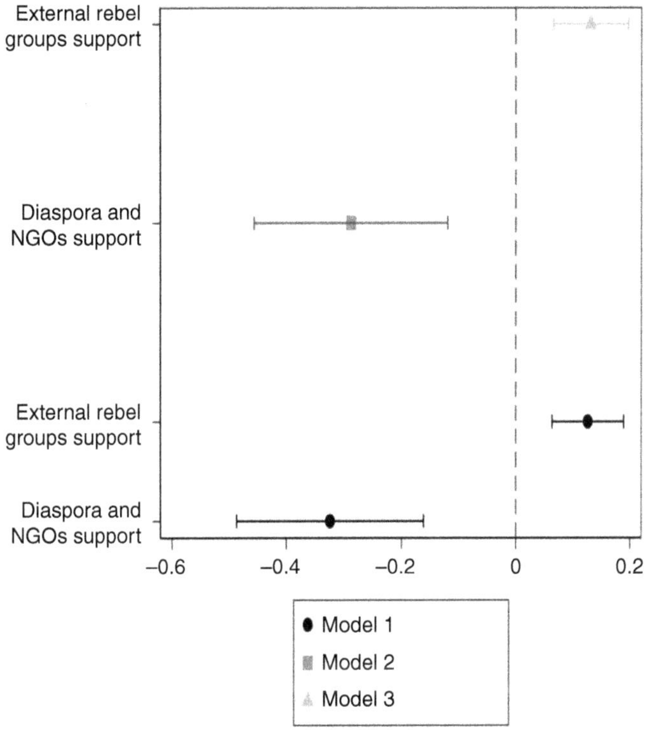

Figure A.6 Marginal effects of the variables of interest on the expected lethality of terrorism (binomial models from Figure 5.5).

Note: The horizontal lines represent 95% confidence intervals.

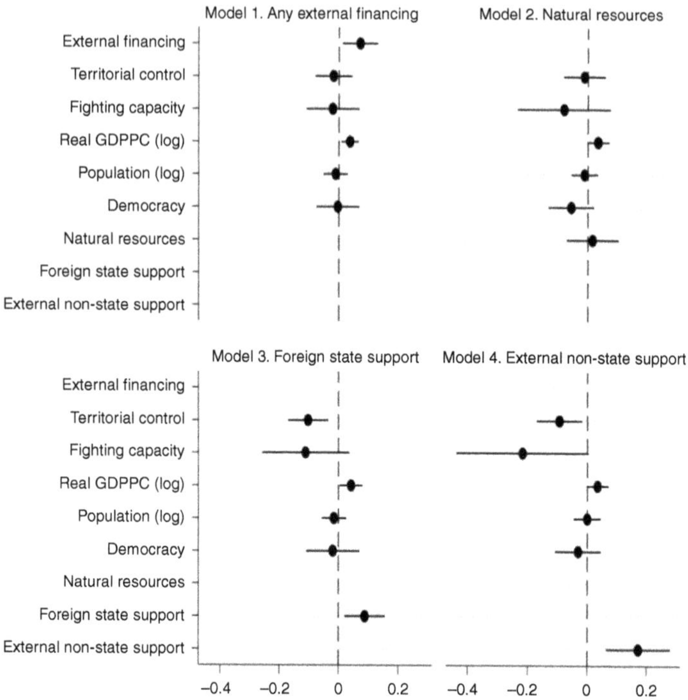

Figure A.7 The effect of external financing on the likelihood of lethality of terrorism (OLS as alternative functional form).

Note: The horizontal lines represent 95% confidence intervals.

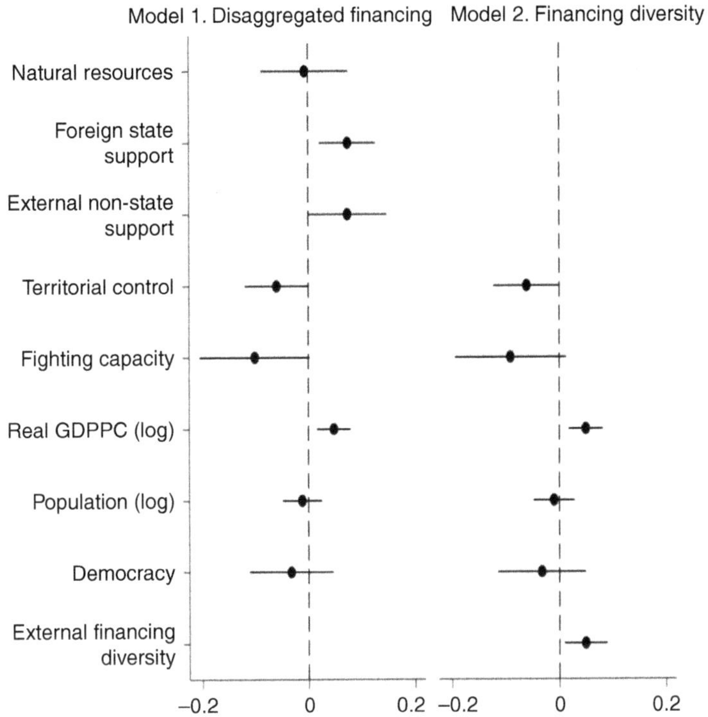

Figure A.8 Effects of different types of external financing and external financing diversity on likelihood of lethality of terrorism (OLS as alternative functional form).

Note: The horizontal lines represent 95% confidence intervals.

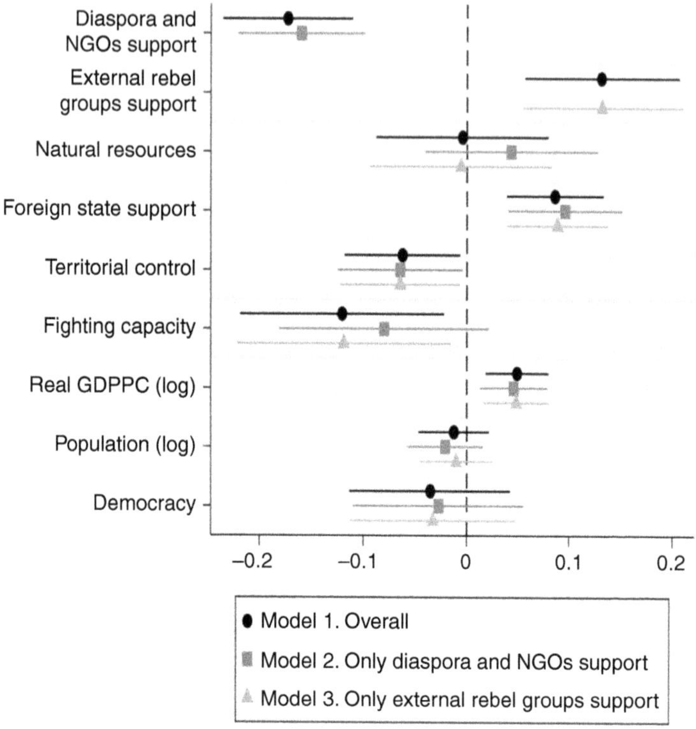

Figure A.9 The effect of types of external non-state supporters on terrorism intensity (OLS as alternative functional form).

Note: The horizontal lines represent 95% confidence intervals.

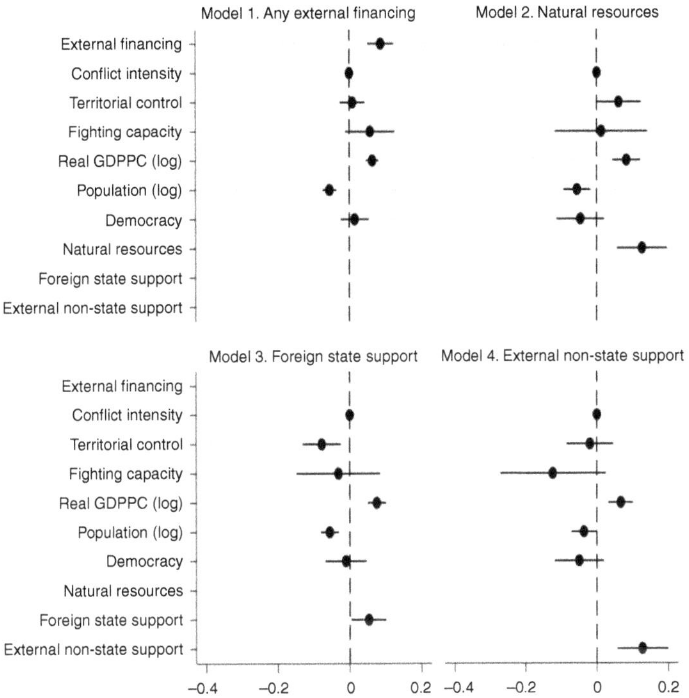

Figure A.10 The effect of external financing on the likelihood of terrorism occurrence (logit functional form).

Note: The horizontal lines represent 95% confidence intervals.

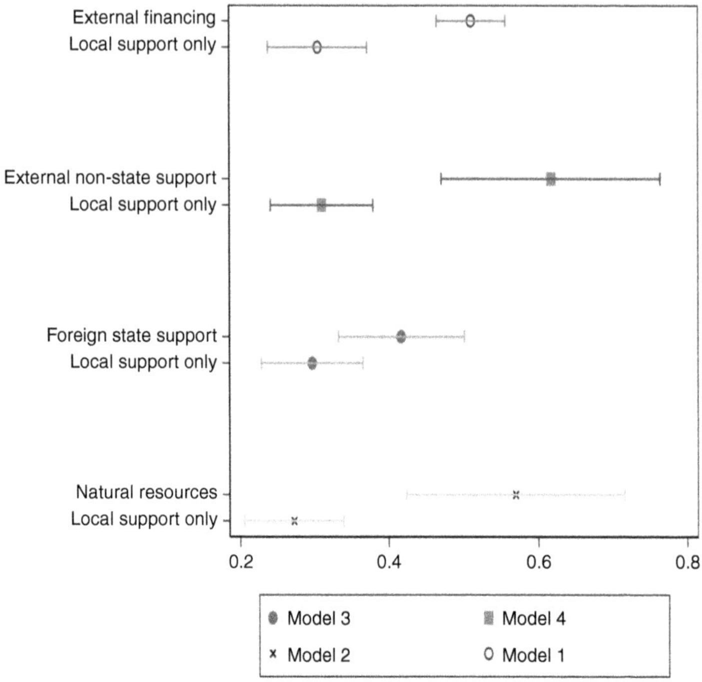

Figure A.11 Marginal effects of the variables of interest on the likelihood of terrorism occurrence (logit functional form from Figure 3).

Note: The horizontal lines represent 95% confidence intervals.

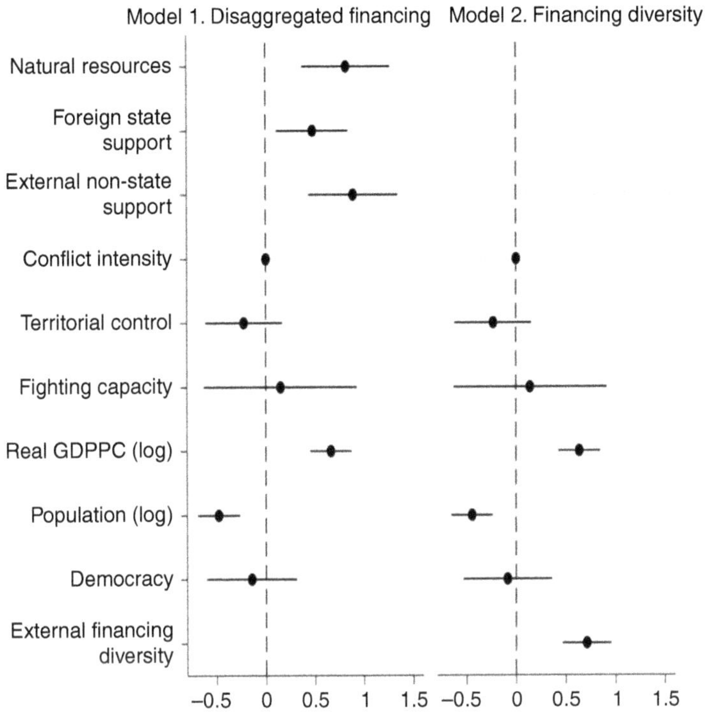

Figure A.12 Effects of different types of external financing and external financing diversity on the likelihood of terrorism occurrence (logit functional form).

Note: The horizontal lines represent 95% confidence intervals.

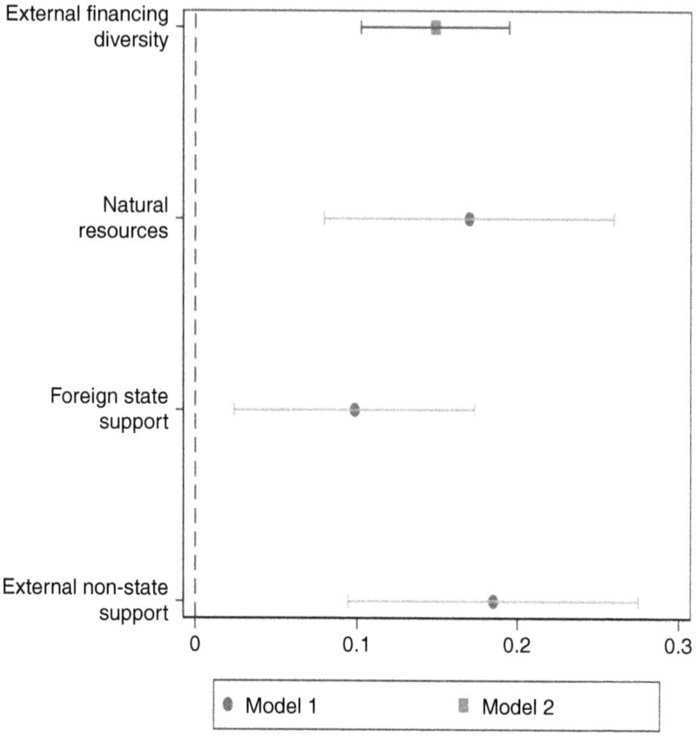

Figure A.13 Marginal effects of the variables of interest on the likelihood of terrorism occurrence (logit functional form from Figure 5).

Note: The horizontal lines represent 95% confidence intervals.

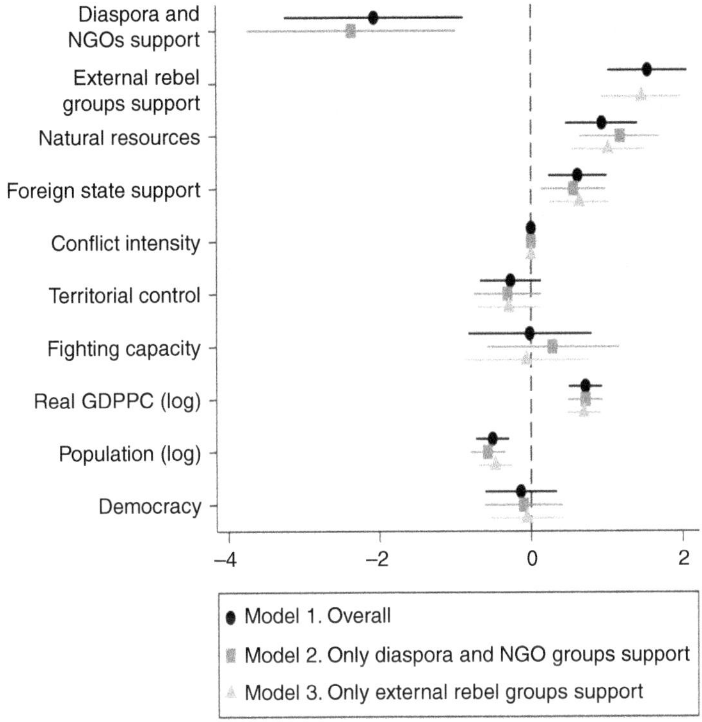

Figure A.14 The effect of types of external non-state supporters on the likelihood of terrorism occurrence (logit functional form).

Note: The horizontal lines represent 95% confidence intervals.

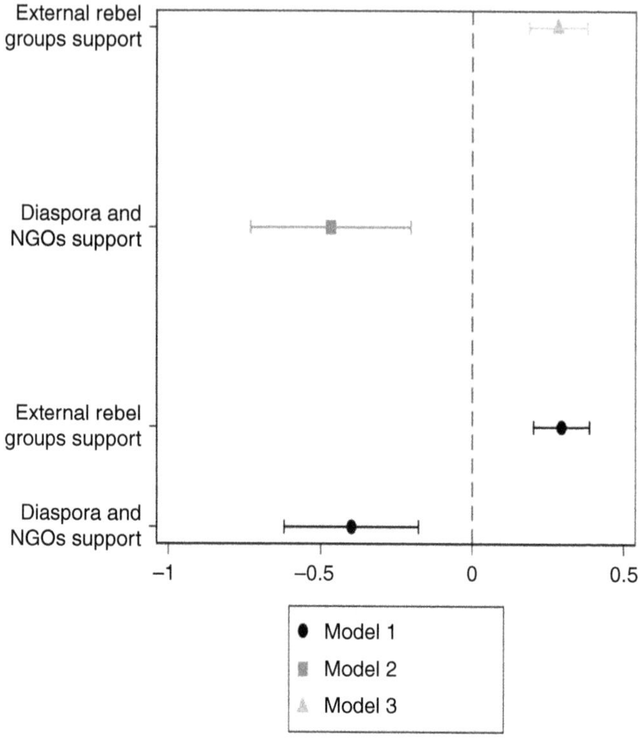

Figure A.15 Marginal effects of the variables of interest on the likelihood of terrorism occurrence (logit functional form from Figure 7).

Note: The horizontal lines represent 95% confidence intervals.

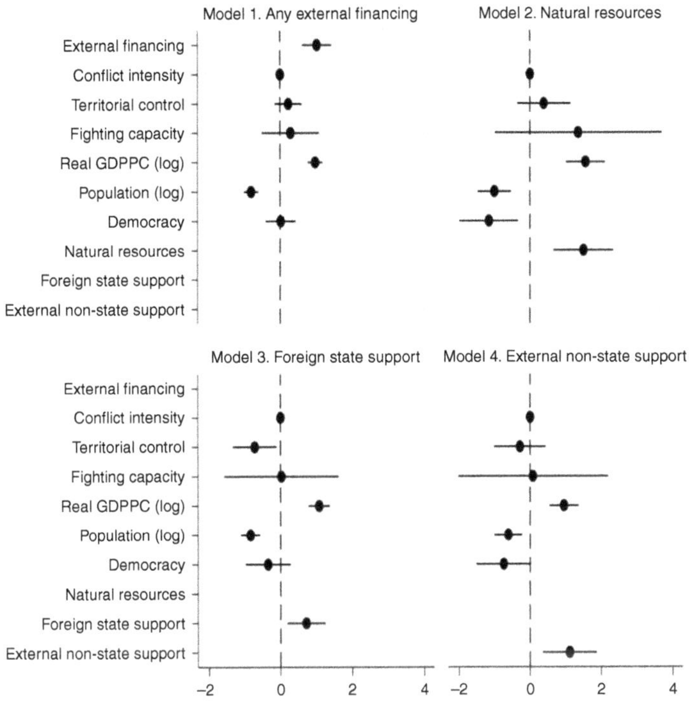

Figure A.16 The effect of external financing on the likelihood of highly destructive explosive (logit functional form).

Note: The horizontal lines represent 95% confidence intervals.

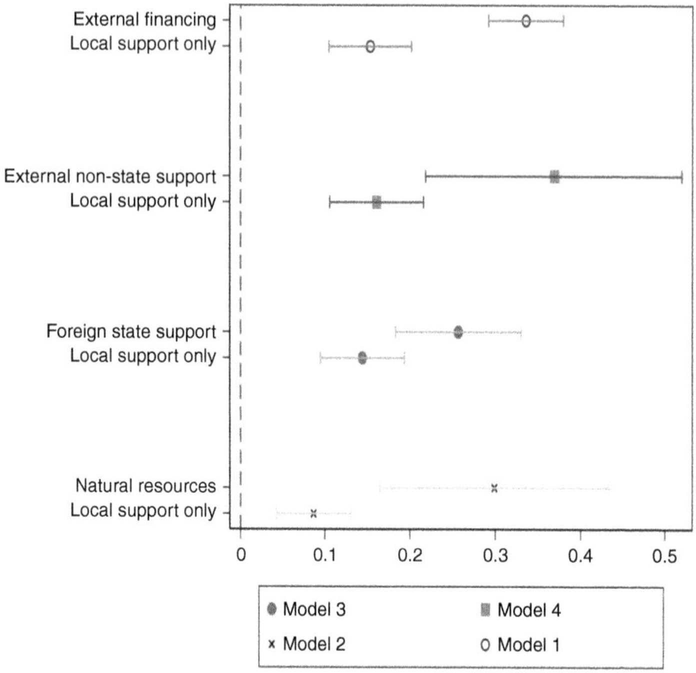

Figure A.17 Marginal effects of the variables of interest on the likelihood of highly destructive explosive (logit functional form from Figure 10).

Note: The horizontal lines represent 95% confidence intervals.

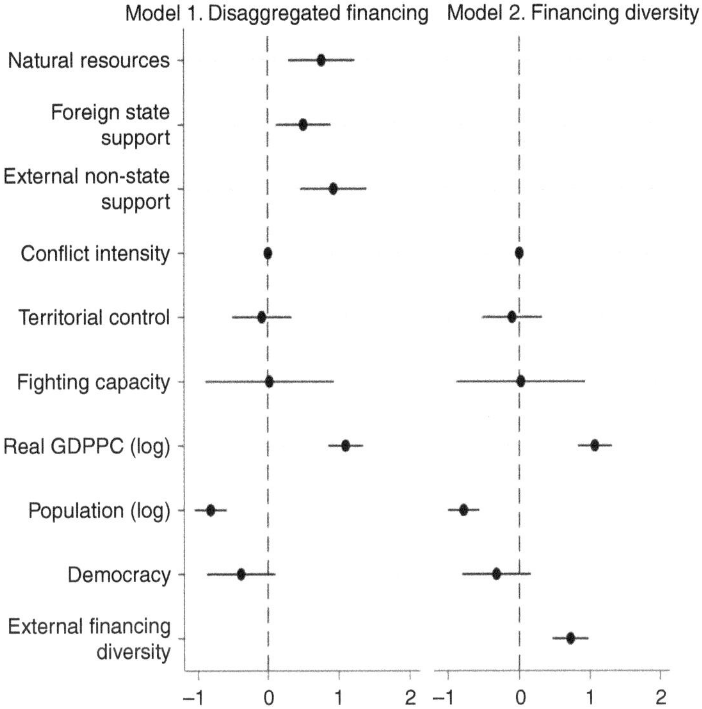

Figure A.18 The overall effect of types of external financing and external financing diversity on the likelihood of highly destructive explosive (logit functional form).

Note: The horizontal lines represent 95% confidence intervals.

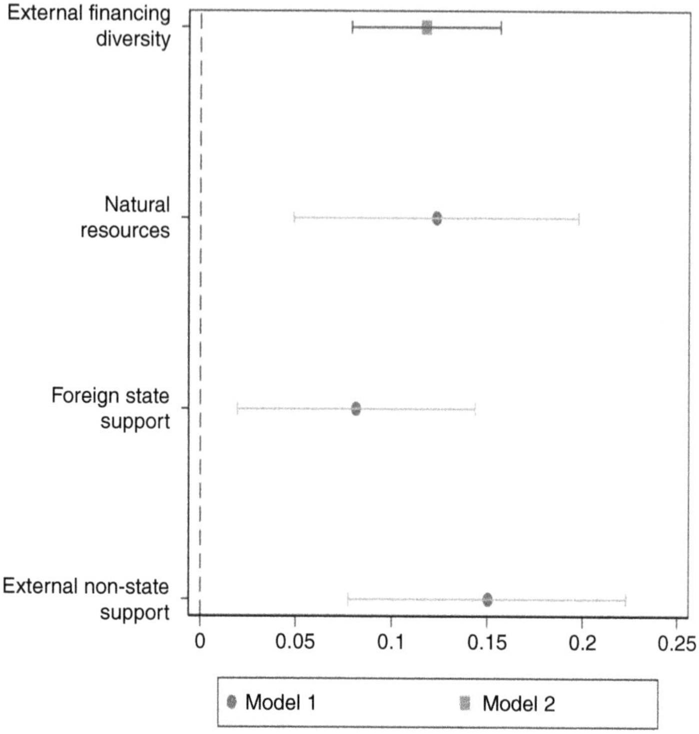

Figure A.19 Marginal effects of the variables of interest on the likelihood of highly destructive explosive (logit functional form from Figure 5).

Note: The horizontal lines represent 95% confidence intervals.

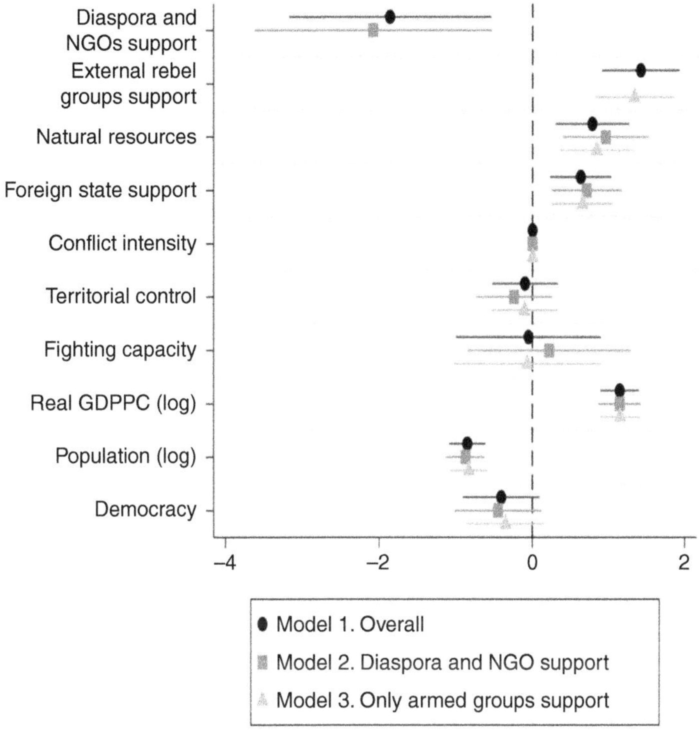

Figure A.20 The effect of types of external non-state supporters on the likelihood of highly destructive explosive (logit functional form).

Note: The horizontal lines represent 95% confidence intervals.

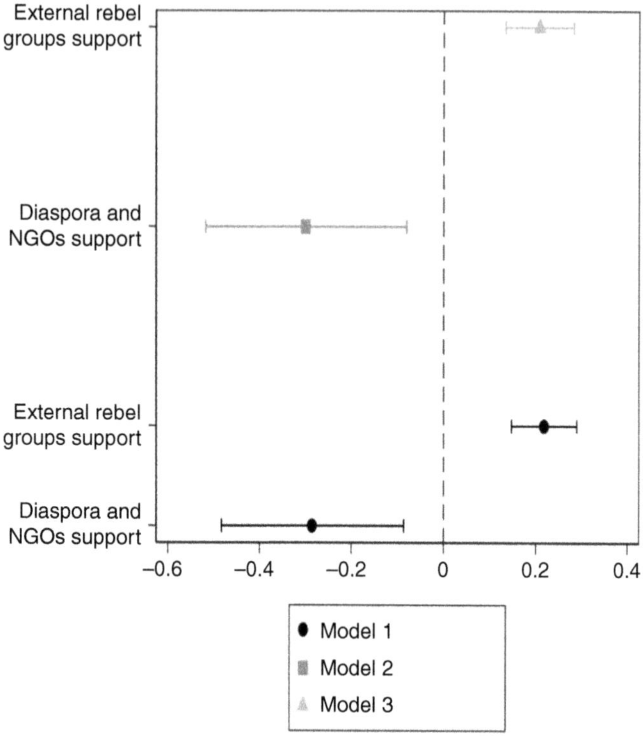

Figure A.21 Marginal effects of the variables of interest on the likelihood on the likelihood of highly destructive explosive (logit functional form from Figure 7).

Note: The horizontal lines represent 95% confidence intervals.

Index

Note: Page numbers in *italic* refers to figures.

For Product Safety Concerns and Information please contact our EU representative GPSR@taylorandfrancis.com
Taylor & Francis Verlag GmbH, Kaufingerstraße 24, 80331 München, Germany

www.ingramcontent.com/pod-product-compliance
Ingram Content Group UK Ltd.
Pitfield, Milton Keynes, MK11 3LW, UK
UKHW022157190926
475702UK00003B/76
* 9 7 8 1 0 3 2 4 4 5 0 1 4 *